THE
The Su
BABY HACKS GUIDE FOR MEN

Level Up Your Parenting Game for Baby's First Year with 100+ Expert Strategies, Tips, and Hacks

MADDOX & FLORA KING

Copyright © 2024 Parentlnk Press
All rights reserved.

This book's content may not be reproduced, duplicated, or transmitted without explicit written permission from the author or publisher.

Under no circumstances shall the publisher, author, or anyone else be held responsible for any blame, legal liability, damages, reparation, or monetary loss arising from the information in this book, either directly or indirectly.

Legal Notice:

This book is protected by copyright and is intended for personal use only. Any alteration, distribution, sale, use, quotation, or paraphrasing of any part or content within this book requires the consent of the author or publisher.

Disclaimer Notice:

The information in this document is provided for educational and entertainment purposes only. Every effort has been made to present accurate, up-to-date, reliable, and complete information, but no warranties of any kind are declared or implied. Readers should be aware that the author is not providing legal, financial, medical, or professional advice.

By reading this document, the reader agrees that the author is not responsible under any circumstances for any direct or indirect losses resulting from the use of the information contained within, including, but not limited to, errors, omissions, or inaccuracies.

CONTENTS

Part One
SETTING THE STAGE FOR SUCCESS

Chapter One
FROM ZERO TO PARENTHOOD: THE EPIC SAGA OF MONTH ONE IN DADVILLE (MONTH 1) 8

Chapter Two
GROWTH SPURTS AND GRINS: THE PLAYBOOK FOR DAD'S NEXT CHAPTER (MONTHS 2-3) 47

Chapter Three
CRAWLING AND CUDDLES: A DAD'S GUIDE TO THE MOBILE MONTHS (MONTHS 4-6) 66

Chapter Four
LITTLE EXPLORER, BIG DISCOVERIES: NAVIGATING THE SEVEN-TO NINE-MONTH ADVENTURE IN DADHOOD (MONTHS 7-9) 82

Chapter Five
BRIDGING THE BABY GAP: MASTERING MILESTONES IN THE LAST LAP OF YEAR ONE (MONTHS 10-12) 95

Chapter Six
LITTLE PERSON, BIG FEELINGS: CULTIVATING EMOTIONAL INTELLIGENCE IN YOUR BABY'S FIRST YEAR 109

Part Two
BE THE BEST DAD YOU CAN BE

Chapter Seven
FROM TWO TO THREE: A DAD'S GUIDE TO HARMONIZING FAMILY AND RELATIONSHIP 124

Chapter Eight
BABY ON BOARD: A DAD'S GUIDE TO GETTING OUT OF THE HOUSE WITH A BABY 135

Chapter Nine
TROUBLESHOOTING GUIDE FOR DAD CHALLENGES 146

Conclusion
THE END OF THE BOOK BUT NOT YOUR JOURNEY 164

BIBLIOGRAPHY 167

Get Your Free Bonuses Now!

BONUS # 1: Survival Checklists for Dads
Your Key to Staying Organized and Making the Pregnancy Journey Super Smooth!

BONUS # 2: Mental Wellness Guide for Dads
Your Indispensable Guide to Self-care and Self-discovery, Ensuring a Journey Towards a Happier and More Fulfilled You!

BONUS # 3: Meditation Audio for Dads
Your Instant Escape to Calmness, Relaxation, and Well-deserved Quality "Me Time."

Scan with your phone's camera **OR** go to: https://bit.ly/43nFe2P

There I stood, covered in poop, while my baby chilled on the changing mat for the first time in ages. She hadn't pooped in three days and was very vocal about the state of her stomach. I didn't even know babies could go that long without pooping, especially considering the pooptastic display she had given us her first week at home. But the screaming let us know that she was uncomfortable, and only a baby sling would calm her down. I was on diaper duty before her nightly sling snooze, when my daughter let rip with the most explosive display I'd seen since my college parties.

There was poop everywhere. No one tells you about the complexities of a baby's bowel movements, or that there is a 100% chance you and everything nearby will end up splattered with your sweet angel's butt juice. Too graphic? Absolutely. That's exactly the way it should be. You've entered your first year of fatherhood, which is only the start of the explosive behavior you're in store for.

Hearing my cry of shock and panic, Flora rushed in to see what the problem was. We had never laughed that hard. There was our sweet baby, lying in her own excrement, completely content. This was a core memory I often thought about as we journeyed through parenthood.

Going through pregnancy and birth is one thing, but being a father is something else altogether. You're responsible for keeping another human alive, and the weight of that responsibility is unreal. Nothing prepares you for how fatherhood will change how you see the world and your partner. If you thought pregnancy was a rollercoaster, wait for the first year of fatherhood. It feels sort of like building a massive puzzle without having the picture on the box as a guide. It's overwhelming and confusing, and everyone builds their puzzle differently, so their advice only gets you so far. The sleepless nights, diaper changes, feeding schedules, soothing techniques, and myriad of emotions that come with caring for a newborn are all pieces you'll struggle to figure out. But don't worry! It's all a normal part of the new dad process.

You'll likely have loads of questions:

How can I be a good wingman if my partner is breastfeeding?
What's the best option if breastfeeding isn't in the cards?
How do I survive the sleep-deprived phase?
Are there any tricks for calming a fussy baby?
How will this change my friendships and socializing?
What's the secret to keeping the romance alive?

There will probably be hundreds more, as well.

Then, your baby will start hitting milestones, and you'll finally remember to pack the extra diapers and the bottle they love. Slowly, the pieces will begin to fit together. Each day of that first year, you'll find a new puzzle piece. It might be the first smile, the first steps, or even the first coherent babble. Each piece you fit together creates a beautiful picture of your growing baby, and you slowly find the answers to all of your questions.

Just like in a complex puzzle, there will be moments when the experience is overwhelming. Sleepless nights, teething troubles, and the constant demand for attention may make it feel like some pieces just don't fit. I've been there, and I know how frustrating it can be. But fatherhood doesn't happen all at once. It's made up of moments of pure joy and utter despair, and sometimes you experience both in the span of a few minutes. You aren't supposed to finish the puzzle in a day. It's something you work on, tinker with, and ponder for years.

The first year of your child's life is a transformative journey for your family. You will learn what sacrifice means and figure out the best way to compromise and meet everyone's needs. You will experience fear in a new way as you watch your baby explore the world around them, usually in the most hazardous way possible. But most of all, you will learn what it means to love—the kind of love that fills you up and has you thinking crazy thoughts (like having more babies).

How do I know all this? My name is Maddox King, and I've done this three times already. I'm a software engineer—someone who gets off on solving puzzles—but fatherhood was one puzzle that really threw me. There was no code to crack, because each baby popped out and immediately threw us a curveball. Each first year with our kids had me scratching my head and rethinking my strategies. Yes, some things worked with all three children, and I'll share all of those tips and tricks with you. But each of my kids is unique, and that meant that there were aspects of fatherhood that I experienced for the first time, each time around.

After doing the dad thing for a few years, I've had my fair share of discoveries that have made parenting easier, and also helped me see just how vital dads are. Nothing can really prepare you for what's coming, but, as cliche as it sounds, knowledge is power. Arming yourself with tips, tricks, and strategies can help you develop a solid base to work from and fall back on as you navigate this new chapter of life.

This book is more than just a dry guide of what milestones you can expect in the first year. It's a manual distilled from years of experience, research, and mistakes. With three kids, I've covered a lot of the major "Oh, my God" moments of fatherhood. I believe that, with the right support, you can get through yours, too.

Did you know that becoming a dad actually changes your brain? Your brain increases connections, influencing affection, threat detection, and problem-solving. But a dad's brain, unlike a mom's, has peak activity in the neocortex, which relates to pushing boundaries and social interaction. That means you offer your child something unique as you develop your relationship with them.

What sets this book apart is the fact that it's created with your dad's brain in mind. It's a helpful resource as you assemble the pieces that make up your unique fathering experience. Each chapter also includes a woman's perspective, so you get some helpful inside info, too. Plus, each time you see a #, you know that you are getting one of the 100+ tips and tricks to give you the edge you need to be a superdad.

This book will make you laugh, help you when you cry (trust me, it's coming), and provide a judgment-free perspective on common first-time dad experiences. The fact that I found bathing a slippery newborn practically impossible might not help you directly, but my solution (wearing gloves) could help you see that ingenuity, humor, and pure survival instinct are crucial components in your first year of fatherhood.

There is no magic pill for fatherhood, but there are helpful resources, like this book, that can give you solid strategies, advice, and hacks to support you until you can figure out what works best for your family.

Parenting is tough, but it doesn't have to be lonely. Each family may be working on their own puzzle, but we can all share tips and swap strategies. I know how daunting it feels to face fatherhood with all its unknowns, so let's get started together, one piece at a time.

Part One
SETTING THE STAGE FOR SUCCESS

Chapter One
FROM ZERO TO PARENTHOOD: THE EPIC SAGA OF MONTH ONE IN DADVILLE (MONTH 1)

"Labor and delivery is measured in hours. Birth is a moment. Being a parent is the rest of your life."
— *Lisa Marshall*

This is it—one of the most profound and memorable moments of your life is about to happen, and nothing I can say is going to prepare you for it. Don't panic, though! What you're feeling is completely normal.

Your partner is in labor, and fear may be your primary emotion. I remember watching Flora bravely breathe through those first contractions, and I thought, "We've got this." Flora certainly did, but my anxiety levels skyrocketed as the contractions got worse.

The latent stage of labor was manageable. Her cervix was softening, and the contractions were strong but irregular. I made sure she had snacks and stayed hydrated. But the first stage of labor had me freaking out more than I thought I would. Nothing prepares you for seeing your partner in that much pain. I felt helpless as the contractions rolled in thick and fast. All I could do was help Flora change positions, get her ice chips, and rub her back. I gave her as much support as I could, and tried to internalize my rising panic.

This was the moment we'd been waiting for. Nine months of prep work had culminated in this terrifying, overwhelming, exciting moment. Our daughter's birth wasn't quite what we had planned. She was breech, and Flora needed a C-section. Although I was anxious on the inside, being familiar with what a C-section was helped me be the supportive partner Flora needed.

And then, in the crisp and somewhat antiseptic air of the delivery room, I watched the miracle of my baby girl's first breath. All I can say is that you should definitely expect tears. Some of the toughest guys I know have been laid low by the sight and sound of their babies—and that's the way it should be. Watching your baby make their debut into the world is a big, emotional moment. Embrace it. Washington Irving once said, "There is a sacredness in tears. They are not the mark of weakness, but of power." The emotions you feel looking at your new baby are a testament to the power of the moment and how profoundly it has changed your life. Your tears represent love, relief, and commitment.

What comes next may be a bit of a blur. Your partner will be attended to, and your baby will be tested and cleaned up a bit. But then comes the Golden Hour. This is a time when you can establish a connection with your baby through skin-to-skin contact. Research shows that bare-skinned cuddles help regulate your baby's temperature and heart rate (Widström et al., 2019). You probably haven't thought about how stressful birth is for a baby, but skin-to-skin contact in the hour after birth can help mitigate some of that stress.

It's pretty cool knowing that one of your baby's first sensory experiences is the touch and smell of your skin. Be as present as possible during this time. Ignore the messages from friends and family and just be in the moment with your partner and baby. Some of the best advice I got was not to be frightened. When they place that tiny bundle of baby on your chest, you'll feel clumsy, but your baby won't break. Just be gentle and breathe.

The following 48 hours will be a whirlwind. You'll let family and friends know you're a dad, and decide whether you want visitors. Some hospitals only allow limited visitors, so decide who will be on the list. You may not want visitors at all, which is entirely your prerogative. Don't let family strongarm you into seeing the baby if you and your partner want to keep your time in the hospital private.

Although this time is busy, you'll also feel a bit useless. The hospital staff will be caring for your baby and your partner, so there won't be much for you to do. But don't be afraid to ask questions and video record demonstrations of proper baby-handling techniques. You'll have access to maternity nurses who can give you pro tips on bathing, swaddling, and how many wet diapers to look out for. Make the most of the opportunity to pick their brains and shore up as many helpful hints as possible.

Getting Home

You may think leaving the hospital and getting home to your own space is the best thing ever, but trust me, it can be way more stressful than you expect. Again, park the panic. You've got this. Babies are hardy little critters. When you strap them into the car seat, the buckle will look huge, and you'll triple check that you installed the thing correctly, but everything will be okay. Your dad instincts are already kicking in.

I clearly remember Flora and me arriving home with our daughter. She sat in the car seat in the middle of the living room. We both stared at each other, wondering what the hell was supposed to happen next. Then she started screaming, and the fun began.

Although the hospital is busy and exhausting, it feels safe. There is a team of people on hand to help when your baby cries, and you can try to catch a power nap since you know that someone will keep an eye on your baby. But once you're home, you're on your own.

I know it's intimidating, but I'll let you in on a secret: Your baby already thinks you're the best thing ever. They love how you smell and the way your big hands make them feel safe. You are the center of their world, and will be for years to come.

Eat, Sleep, Cry, Poop, Repeat...Or Is It?

New dad responsibilities can feel like a lot. It's easy to get ahead of yourself and start freaking out about everything. But it's not babygeddon, like you may have been led to believe. The reality is that those first few days and weeks are pretty monotonous. All those things you're worrying about probably won't happen for a few months, at least.

I remember standing in line at the grocery store holding a cabbage (more on that later) when the elderly man in front of me smiled kindly and asked how old my baby was. "I know the look of a tired dad, son. By the way, the cabbage leaves should do the trick." I must admit, I felt pretty emotional. The haze of new fatherhood was thick, and for the first time since having my daughter, I felt seen. After making small talk and shuffling toward the register, Arthur, the kindly gentleman, casually dropped some new dad advice that saved my sanity. And now I'm going to share it with you.

#1 - Keep your baby's world small.

They've been cozy in your partner's womb, insulated from loud noises, fluctuating temperatures, and strange faces. But now they're on the outside, and it's a lot.

Arthur told me to keep things as simple as possible. "Son," he said, "they eat, sleep, cry, and poop, and you just need to figure out that rhythm. But it's hard to do that if you're busy and you don't give your baby and yourselves the space you need to get to know each other."

Mind blown.

It was like this advice from a stranger gave me permission to say no to family, social engagements, and anything we didn't have the emotional capacity for. And that's precisely what we did. We hibernated for those first few weeks and basked in the joy, love, and sleeplessness that comes with a new baby. We gave ourselves the gift of space, and you might want to do so, as well.

Family Expectations

Your new baby is a big deal, and friends and family are sure to be excited. But that excitement can put pressure on you and your partner that you don't need. The best way to manage everyone's expectations is clear communication and clearly defined boundaries.

Create a Visiting Roster

You get to choose who comes to visit, and when. Set aside visiting times when friends and family can come over.

Ask for Specific Help

Your nearest and dearest want to help, and you'll need it, so be specific and let them know how they can support you. Maybe that's by washing dishes, bringing dinner, or doing the laundry. My sister did the grocery shopping for us for the first month, helping us prepare for our pre-planned meals. She would also take care of the laundry and load the dishwasher when she dropped the groceries off. It was such a help, and meant fewer mental gymnastics for us when we didn't have the brainpower.

Set Clear Boundaries

Be honest and upfront with loved ones. If you don't want visitors during the first few weeks, create a group chat with your family and friends. You can share baby photos and updates without having to actually have anyone in your space. Believe me, your partner will appreciate the privacy. She will feel like an exhausted, oozing mess in those early days, and may struggle to find time to shower, let alone entertain guests.

You also need to have crucial conversations about who can hold your baby and what precautions you want them to take. Your baby's immune system is still developing, so you might ask friends and family to be up to date on routine vaccinations, including TDAP and flu shots. Hand-washing is also a must. You can make it easier by having a good hand soap in your bathroom. You can even greet guests with hand sanitizer at the door.

Postpartum Recovery

I wish I had known more about what the postpartum period would look like for Flora. I knew about the sleepless nights and diapers, but hadn't really considered the logistics of recovery from a C-section.

It was painful for her to get off the sofa, and she was frustrated that she couldn't respond to our daughter as quickly as she would have liked. After watching her struggle, I made up a care basket. It had breast pads, nipple cream, a water bottle, snacks, magazines, her Kindle, and a burp cloth. Having the essentials with her meant she didn't have to move around as much. Plus, I could bring our daughter to her.

If your partner had a vaginal birth, she may have stitches or need perineal care. An easy hack for helping your partner is to run a sitz bath with Epsom salt. The salt helps her sensitive bits heal quicker.

#2 - Don't let her put salt water on her breasts. The salt will dry out her nipples and make them more susceptible to cracking. Trust me, this is one part of breastfeeding your partner can do without.

You can also get her a donut pillow to sit on rather than putting pressure on an area that's been through a lot already.

Your partner's body has been through a massive change, and she probably won't feel like herself. Chances are, she's self-conscious and overwhelmed with the changes. It's your job to remind her that she is beautiful and loved.

Here are some easy tips to help you support your postpartum partner:

#3 - Be on baby duty and make time for your partner to shower.

#4 - Keep the laundry up to date so she has clean clothes and bed linens.

#5 - Stockpile breast pads and maternity pads so your partner has the essentials she needs.

#6 - Set up a cozy nursing or feeding station with essentials like water, snacks, burp cloths, and entertainment.

#7 - Run interference and shield your partner from unnecessary stressors.

Understanding Postpartum Depression (PPD)

Postpartum depression is a real and scary situation for new moms. So many women are caught up in the chaos of caring for their new babies that they miss the important warning signs that they're not okay. While it's normal for new moms to experience mood swings and feelings of overwhelm, PPD is like getting stuck in a loop of sadness, anxiety, and hopelessness that doesn't seem to end. One out of seven women experiences PPD, usually one to three weeks after giving birth.

PPD warning signs can include:

- Feeling sad, emotional, fragile, or angry, even when things are going okay.
- Withdrawing from friends and family.

- Struggling to sleep, even when she's exhausted.
- Losing her appetite.
- Feelings of guilt and inadequacy as a mother.
- Frequent headaches or stomach aches.

How can you help?

Be supportive and understanding: Let your partner know that you're there for her, no matter what. Offer a listening ear, a shoulder to cry on, and reassurance that she's not alone in this.

Help her look after herself: Take over baby duty so she can nap, go for a walk, or chat with a friend.

#8 - Make her snacks and meals, so she has one less thing to think about. Or, run her a bath while you put the baby to bed.

Help with household chores: Take on more household responsibilities to lighten her load. Whether it's cooking meals, doing laundry, or tidying up the house, every little bit helps. It's just one less thing for her to think about!

Offer practical support: Go with her to doctor's appointments or therapy sessions. PPD needs professional treatment. There is still some stigma around getting help, but simply being there physically and offering emotional support goes a long way.

Be patient and nonjudgmental: Remember that PPD is a medical condition, not a character flaw or a sign of weakness. Help your partner navigate her feelings, reminding her that she is an amazing partner and mother, despite what her brain is telling her.

Figuring Out Feeding

You would think that feeding your baby would be straightforward and simple, since it's nature at its finest, right? Wrong. We both learned the hard way that there is way more to it than just plopping baby on the boob and letting nature run its course. Latch issues, clogged milk ducts, and nighttime feeds are just some of the challenges you've got coming your way. But these challenges don't arrive all at once, and they are all figureoutable.

Take John, for instance. His wife Sarah had dreamed of breastfeeding, but their son was having none of it. John said that Sarah blamed herself, and he struggled having to watch her feel guilty and demoralized. So, he went on a quest to find the best tips and hacks he could to help Sarah on her breastfeeding journey. That's what fatherhood is often about—supporting your partner and baby in any way necessary.

Breastfeeding doesn't always come naturally, so let's look at some common struggles and hacks to help.

Latch Issues

A latch is how your baby takes the nipple and areola into its mouth when feeding. If your baby doesn't have a good latch, feeding can be difficult for both Mom and baby. Our daughter, Natalie, struggled to latch at first, which was frustrating but also hilarious. Flora would keep trying to help her get a good nipple grip, but end up covering our newborn with milk in the process.

#9 - Nipple Sandwich Technique

Encourage your partner to use the "nipple sandwich" technique. Yep, you read that right. You're essentially squashing the breast to make a flatter shape. This makes it easier for the baby to latch onto both the nipple and areola.

#10 - Nipple Shields

A nipple shield fits over your partner's nipple and has small holes that allow milk to flow through. It provides a "harder" nipple, making it easier for your baby to latch. Once your baby has a better latch, your partner can stop using shields.

Clogged Milk Ducts

Milk gets from the breast to your baby via ducts, but sometimes these ducts get clogged (like a drain) and a hard lump forms. A bad latch could be the problem.

#11 - Warm Compress and Massage

A warm compress or a hot bath can help, and so will a gentle massage. Your partner shouldn't stop breastfeeding, because that will only make it worse.

Milk Supply

Your partner is a milk-making machine, but she may need help to keep that machine running.

#12 - Power Pumping

Try power-pumping sessions, where your partner pumps for shorter, more frequent intervals. This sends the signal that more milk is needed, which ups production.

#13 - Use a Haakaa

Your baby may not feed from both breasts during each feeding session. That's where a Haakaa comes in. This is a manual, silicone pump that uses suction to "milk" the breast your baby doesn't feed from. If your partner is producing a lot of milk, it is a great way to stop leaking, prevent clogged milk ducts, and save extra milk.

#14 - Hydration

Fun fact: Breast milk is 90% water. That means drinking water is an easy way to keep up milk supply. But water can get boring, so keep a stash of fruit juice or milk on hand, or spice up the water with herbs, fruit, or cucumber slices.

Mastitis

Mastitis happens when breast tissue gets inflamed, and is common during the first few weeks after birth. Common symptoms include breast pain, milk supply issues, and redness. And that brings us back to me meeting Arthur while holding a cabbage.

#15 - Cabbage Leaves

Cabbage leaves are a decades-old remedy for mastitis, and one of the cheapest ways to treat the condition. Cabbage leaves contain compounds that help reduce inflammation. I have a photo of Flora asleep on the sofa, wearing cabbage leaves, and it's one of my favorite memories from those early days. (Another pro tip is to take candid photos and find joy and humor in the small moments.)

Nighttime Feeds

Waking up throughout the night is normal, but how often your baby wakes up will depend on their digestion rate and waking patterns. Breastfed babies usually feed every two to three hours, while formula-fed babies can go three to four hours. Each feed can last 20 minutes or more, depending on your baby.

It's important to manage your expectations. For a baby, "sleeping through the night" means a five- to six-hour stretch. This doesn't happen until two to three months, at the earliest (and if you're lucky.) That means someone has to be feeding your baby every few hours, and changing their diaper if it's full.

Being Organized

Trust me, you don't want to be caught without a clean bottle when your baby is screaming for food. The frantic scrambling is seriously not worth it.

#16 - Set Up a Bottle Station

Choose a space in your kitchen that won't be in the way, and store your bottle racks and supplies there. You want to keep all your feeding supplies in one area so it's quick and convenient to access them. That includes a drying rack, sterilizer (if you're using one), and tub of all the extra bits.

#17 - Share the Load

If your partner is exclusively breastfeeding, you can help by burping your baby, changing their diaper, and putting them back to sleep.

#18 - Be Strategic

If your partner is pumping, you can do the first feed of the night. For example, we would go to bed at 7:30 p.m. (you laugh now, but just wait), and I would do the 10:30 p.m. feed with a bottle. The next feed would usually be at 01:30 a.m., so Flora would get six hours of sleep. Then we would swap, and Flora would do the second part of the night. Try and work out a schedule that gives you both the most amount of sleep.

Sleep Deprivation, aka Zombie Mode

Picture this: It's 3:00 a.m., and you find yourself stumbling through the darkened halls of your home, guided only by the dim glow of the nightlight in the nursery. Your baby has woken up for the umpteenth time, demanding attention with their tiny cries echoing through the house. As you scoop them up from their crib, you can't help but feel like you're in the midst of a real-life zombie apocalypse.

With heavy eyelids and a foggy mind, you shuffle into the nursery, trying to remember the steps for soothing your little one back to sleep. You fumble through the motions, half-asleep and running on pure parental instinct, as if you've been transformed into a sleep-deprived zombie desperately seeking sustenance (or, in this case, a few precious hours of uninterrupted sleep).

As you rock your baby back and forth, you catch a glimpse of yourself in the mirror and can't help but chuckle at the sight. Your hair is a mess, your eyes are bloodshot, and there's a distinct possibility that you've accidentally put your shirt on inside out. But, in that moment, all that matters is soothing your little one and coaxing them back to sleep, even if it means embracing your inner zombie and stumbling through the night in a sleep-deprived haze.

With a weary sigh and a silent prayer for a few hours of peace, you settle into the rocking chair and continue your zombie-like shuffle through the endless cycle of feedings, diaper changes, and midnight cuddles—because, as any new parent will tell you, sometimes the only way to survive the zombie apocalypse is with a healthy dose of humor and a whole lot of love.

The first three months of parenthood are brutal when it comes to sleep. By the end of the second week, Flora and I could barely string two sentences together, which made for some hilarious conversations. According to the Montreal Children's Hospital, new parents lose around 400 hours of sleep in their first year of parenthood.

You'll wake up when your baby cries or needs to feed, but what people don't tell you is that you'll also wake up just to check that they're breathing. And even when you try to take a nap, you may be too wired and overtired to actually sleep.

We'll explore more sleep strategies later in the chapter, but here are some quick hacks you can start using right now (because I know you're getting desperate):

#19 - Audit your sleep hygiene. Are your linens clean? Is your room dark? Are you doom scrolling for an hour instead of going to bed? Did you drink six cups of coffee? Better sleep starts with better habits.

#20 - Say "No." To what, you ask? Anything and everything that sucks your energy and takes up unnecessary time. These early weeks are all about survival, and this is the one time you get to be selfish.

#21 - Create a bedtime routine. You might as well get used to a more routine way of doing things, because kids need routines to thrive. Try to stick to the same bedtime, and develop the same rhythm an hour before bed. A bath, hot shower, a book, whatever—just skip screens, because they will suck you in and keep you up.

#22 - Get some sunlight on your eyeballs. Natural light in the morning helps regulate your circadian rhythm, and can even improve the sleep you do get (Blume et al., 2019).

#23 - Drink water. According to the Sleep Foundation, sleep deprivation may cause dehydration (Suni & Suni, 2024). The problem is that dehydration also makes you more tired. So, choose a glass of water over the coffee you're probably sipping on.

Newborn Care - The Basics of Keeping Baby Alive

In the early days of parenthood, keeping our newborn baby alive felt like the ultimate survival mission. It was a delicate balance of feeding, changing, and soothing, all while grappling with the overwhelming fear of somehow getting it wrong.

One night, in a sleep-deprived haze, I found myself staring down at my tiny baby, wondering if I was up to the task. What if I didn't burp her properly? What if, heaven forbid, I accidentally put her diaper on backward?

But as I held her close and felt her tiny heartbeat against my chest, I realized something profound. Despite my fears and insecurities, there was one thing I knew for certain: I would move mountains, conquer dragons, and brave the fiercest storms to keep my precious baby safe and sound.

Armed with nothing but love, determination, and a healthy dose of caffeine, I embarked on the adventure of parenthood, one sleepless night and one dirty diaper at a time. When it comes to keeping your newborn baby alive, sometimes all you can do is take a deep breath, trust your instincts, and hold on for dear life.

Diaper-Changing Duties

Your baby will pee and poop…a lot. In fact, you can expect about six wet diapers and three poops per day. The good news is that you'll become a diaper pro in no time. Diapers are one thing you can step up and help with, to give your recovering partner a chance to rest.

#24 - **Keep the changing table stocked with:**

- Diapers
- Wipes

- Diaper rash cream
- Spare clothes
- Hand towel

I also had a mobile changing station that I kept stocked. It was a basket with all the same essentials and a changing mat. The spare clothes and hand towel are for the inevitable poop explosions. You can also take the initiative (major brownie points) and keep the diaper bag locked and loaded.

Here are some diaper bag essentials:

- Diapers and wipes
- Diaper rash cream
- Plastic bags
- Changing mat
- Extra onesies
- Burp cloths
- Feeding essentials (like a bottle and breast pads)
- Pacifiers
- Baby blanket
- Hat and sunscreen
- Emergency information card
- Snacks and a water bottle (for you and Mom)

You can also take over the nighttime diaper changes if your partner exclusively breastfeeds.

#25 - **Keep diaper changes quick and low-key.** You want dim lights and no unnecessary stimulation so your baby goes back to sleep quickly. Try warming the wipes, because nothing freaks out a newborn at night more than a cold, wet wipe.

Breastfeeding, Formula, and Finding Your Feeding Rhythm

In the early days of parenthood, finding our feeding rhythm with our newborn felt like a chaotic dance of trial and error. With each hungry cry or squirming wiggle, we stumbled through the steps, trying to decode the signals and meet our baby's needs.

At first, it was a whirlwind of uncertainty and exhaustion. We juggled bottles and breast pumps, trying to remember which side we nursed on last or how many ounces we had warmed up. We stumbled through the night, bleary-eyed and delirious, as we navigated the uncharted waters of newborn feeding schedules.

But gradually, as we settled into our roles as parents, something miraculous happened: We began to find our rhythm, like a well-choreographed duet between parent and child. We learned to anticipate our baby's hunger cues and to recognize the subtle signs of contentment after a satisfying feed.

Fun fact: Your baby grows more in the first year than at any other time.

Keeping your baby fed is probably the most time-consuming activity during those early weeks, especially if you are going with on-demand feeding. What's that, you ask? It just means that you follow your baby's cues in the early weeks and feed them whenever they show signs of hunger.

What signs?

Don't worry, I've got you covered.

If your baby starts rooting around on your chest or neck, sucking their hands, or is fussier than usual, chances are they're hungry.

Creating a feeding schedule with a breastfed baby is tricky, because you have to follow their hunger and fullness cues. But if you are formula-feeding, you can work out a more consistent schedule because the formula is more filling and your baby can go three to four hours between feeds.

Here is a rough feeding guide:

Newborn

- 1-2 oz
- 8-12 feeds in 24 hours

1 month

- 2-4 oz
- 6-8 feeds in 24 hours

2 months

- 5-6 oz
- 5-6 feeds in 24 hours

3-5 months

- 6-7 oz
- 5-6 feeds in 24 hours

But how do you know your baby is getting enough food?

Again, it's easier with formula, but there are a few ways you can make sure your baby is filling up on breast milk:

1. Your partner's breasts will feel much softer after a feed. That means the tank is empty.

2. Your baby will start with rapid sucks and then switch to long, rhythmic sucking. While they are sucking rapidly, they are getting foremilk. Foremilk is mainly water, with some nutrients. When your baby starts drinking more deeply, they are getting hindmilk. Hindmilk is thicker and has more calories than foremilk.

3. Finally, they'll be calm, relaxed, and "milk-drunk" after a feed.

Even if you are demand-feeding, your baby will fall into a rhythm, and you can gauge how often they need to eat. If your partner is pumping, you can do some of the feeds with a bottle, giving her time to shower or nap. You can use a baby tracker app or a journal to keep track of feeds to help you establish a feeding routine. You can record feed times, how long they last, and any other observations. Flora and I had a feeding chart that we filled in, making it easier to see when our daughter was going through a growth spurt.

Nighttime feeds are another story, though. The goal is to get as much sleep at night as possible. A calming bedtime routine can really help with that. Flora and I would give our babies a warm bath, a massage, and a feed in a dim room.

But we also had a secret weapon—dream-feeding. We would put the baby to sleep like normal, but, before bed, we would give them a top-up feed. We would leave them swaddled and feed them while they were mostly asleep. It was a quick process, only 5-10 minutes on each side, but it "topped up" their tummy enough for us to get some extra sleep.

Research has found that babies who are given a focal bedtime feed at one month of age tend to sleep for longer stretches at six months (Quante et al., 2022). So, topping up your baby at night now could help them sleep longer later!

I can't tell you what feeding routine will work for you, because each baby is different. I've provided some practical hacks and tips you can use, but a lot of it will come down to you getting to know your baby and their quirks. But regardless of how your routine shapes up, don't look at long or frequent feeds as a bad thing. Use them as special moments to bond with your baby and soak up the newborn snuggles.

What to Do When Your Baby Won't Latch or Feed, or When They Are Fussy

A baby who is fussy about feeding can be majorly stressful, but it's vital that you and your partner stay calm, because your little bundle will sense your tension, and then you're really in for it. There might be some trial and error as you find what works best, but don't lose hope, because you will eventually figure it out.

Check the Feeding Position

Our daughter was struggling to latch and feed properly. We tried everything, and, as a last resort, we took her to a chiropractor. It turned out she was struggling to turn her head on the right side, which made feeding painful and super messy. Sometimes, you just need to find a feeding position that works. Try the football hold, cross-body hold, or side-lying position.

Try Skin-to-Skin Before Feeding

Babies experience a lot, and we have no idea how overstimulating it can be for them. Having skin-to-skin contact before a feed can help your baby feel calmer.

Get Them Interested

Express a bit of milk first to tempt your little one. Our daughter would sometimes rip her mouth off Flora's nipple (a seriously painful experience), but we found that gently massaging and compressing her breast helped with milk flow and kept our daughter interested.

Ask for Help

If you are struggling, get in touch with a lactation consultant. If breastfeeding is important to you and your partner, a professional can help you figure out how to make it happen.

Understanding Your Baby's Different Cries

As new parents, Flora and I often found ourselves playing a guessing game we affectionately dubbed "Cry Roulette." With each whimper, wail, or squawk emanating from our newborn, we would exchange frantic glances, trying to decipher the hidden message behind the cacophony of sounds.

But then, something miraculous happened. In the midst of the chaos, we began to notice subtle differences in our baby's cries—the urgent plea for hunger, the tired sigh of exhaustion, the discomfort of a gassy tummy. It was as if our baby was speaking to us in a secret language, and we were finally starting to understand.

Armed with this newfound knowledge, we embarked on a journey of discovery, learning to decipher the nuances of our baby's cries with each passing day. We became adept at distinguishing between hunger cries and sleepy grumbles, between boredom babbling and colicky wails.

We honed our skills as amateur cry interpreters, and I am going to help you do the same.

Babies cry for all kinds of reasons, but here are some of the most common. You can use this checklist to help you figure out why your baby is upset.

Hunger

A rhythmic, repetitive cry often means hunger. Your baby might also suck on their fists or fingers. If you notice your baby rooting around your chest or turning their head toward the breast or bottle, chances are they were crying for food.

Discomfort

A fussy cry can mean your baby is uncomfortable. They may squirm, arch their back, or kick their legs frantically. The first thing to do is check their diaper. Also, if your baby cries after a feed, they may have an uncomfortable wind and need to be burped.

Tiredness

If your baby is fussy and almost sounds like they are whining, they could be tired. You'll also notice them rubbing their eyes or ears, yawning, or seeming less engaged. An overtired baby may scream and frantically move their arms and legs.

Overstimulation

An intense, high-pitched cry could mean your baby is overstimulated. They will avoid eye contact and turn their head away from you. You may also see jerky movements, and they often arch their back.

Attention

Sometimes, your baby just wants some love and attention—and they often get it with soft whimpering, smiling, and cooing. They'll also reach out for you and make eye contact. Basically, they'll act as cute as possible.

Pain

A sudden, intense cry could indicate that your baby is in pain. They may also clench their fists, arch their back, and make distressed facial expressions.

Gas/Colic

A baby that has gas or colic will cry for a prolonged period of time, and it can be intense. These crying sessions often happen in the late afternoon and evening as your baby struggles to settle. They may also pull their legs up toward their stomachs.

Tips for Responding

- Respond promptly to your baby's cries.
- Cover the basics. Are they tired, hungry, wet, or gassy?
- Try different calming techniques, like rocking, swaying, singing, or gentle patting.

Calming Techniques for Fussy Moments

It was the witching hour, and our baby had transformed into a tiny tornado of tears and tantrums. With each passing moment, the cries grew louder and the wails more desperate, and our frazzled nerves teetered on the brink of collapse. Through trial and so much error, we eventually figured out some top-tier hacks for calming our fussy baby.

The tips below were hard-won over many a meltdown (mine included), but you'll figure out what works for your baby with time.

Swaddling: Some babies love a good swaddle. The tight wrap stops the startle reflex and can make babies feel safe, snug, and secure. It can also help calm an overstimulated baby.

#26 - Velcro swaddles are much easier than no-velcro ones, so give them a try if swaddling isn't your strong suit.

Massage: Physical touch can help lower the levels of stress hormones a fussy baby experiences. Applying firm, gentle, consistent pressure on your baby's body helps calm their autonomous nervous system.

Stroller: The stroller may be your new best friend. It doesn't work for all babies, but sometimes the rocking motion of a stroller can calm a fussy baby and even put them to sleep.

Warm bath: A warm bath in a dimly lit room can be a game-changer for a crying baby. It's not always practical, but it can be effective.

Minimize stimulation: Sometimes, babies just need less of everything. Dim the lights and take them to a quiet room.

Baby wearing: My daughter loved the baby sling. It went everywhere with us because it was almost guaranteed to save us if she was unhappy. There are many excellent baby carrier options available, so you just need to find what works for you.

Feeding: Your baby may not be hungry, but a feed still allows them to be close to you. Babies associate feeding with comfort, and the act of sucking can help calm them.

Pacifier: The choice to use a pacifier (or not) is personal and comes with pros and cons. That being said, they can help soothe and distract a fussy baby.

Get outdoors: Not only does being outside help you relax, it can also help calm your baby. Your baby might actually stop being fussy because you're less stressed. Being outside can also help regulate your child's circadian rhythm. This can help them be less fussy in the afternoon and readier for sleep.

Yoga ball: If pacing with your crying baby gets tedious, try sitting on a yoga ball. The trick with soothing a baby is to avoid jerky movements. A yoga ball lets you move comfortably in soothing motions.

Balancing Work, Personal Life, and Fatherhood During This Intense Period

After weeks of diaper duty, sleepless nights, and endless rounds of baby talk, returning to the office felt like stepping back into a different universe.

But as the days turned into weeks and the weeks into months, I found myself settling into a new rhythm—one that balanced the demands of work with the joys of fatherhood. It wasn't always easy, navigating the competing priorities of deadlines and diaper changes. But with each passing day, I learned to embrace the juggling act with a newfound sense of purpose and determination.

Being overwhelmed with your new family dynamic is normal, but don't worry, it's not forever. You'll find your groove. Balance is also a subjective concept. A balanced life for some dads may seem totally looney for others. Below, I'll give you some practical tips that you might choose to use, but ultimately you need to figure out the best fit for your family.

Be Realistic

You need to be honest about what you can accomplish in a day. Don't overcommit with friends, work, and at home. You might be your family's Superman, but overscheduling is kryptonite.

Time Management

Prioritize tasks. If you find yourself saying, "I don't have time for XYZ," chances are it isn't a priority. We make time for the important things.

Once you have a list of important tasks, break them into manageable chunks. It can be overwhelming looking at everything you have to do, but when you set aside a few minutes for a small part of a task, it's easier to accomplish.

Create a schedule for your day. Having a predictable routine means you have to expend less mental energy. This gives you more time and energy for the things that matter.

Communicate

Communication is an underrated dad skill.

- Chat with your employer about flexible work arrangements, remote work, or adjusted hours. You won't get anywhere if you don't ask.
- Talk with your partner about an equitable home arrangement. If you struggle to juggle your responsibilities, have a conversation and troubleshoot.

Don't Go It Alone

A new baby is a big thing, but there are ways to make it easier! Use a meal delivery service to avoid having to think about dinner, or get weekly groceries delivered to cut out a trip to the store. Flora and I signed up for a baby care subscription box. We got a box of goodies and information on milestones and development to expect each month.

The value of these kinds of services is in the time and mental energy they save. For example, the subscription box automatically adjusted diaper sizes based on our daughter's age, and always included a bonus pack of wipes.

The New Dad Audit: A Week-in-Review Challenge

This challenge encourages self-reflection, goal-setting, and proactive changes to ensure you thrive in your new role as a dad. A new dad named Andrew felt overwhelmed with the responsibility of caring for his wife and newborn, but the New Dad Audit gave him concrete steps to follow and the confidence to be vulnerable and open about the journey.

Day 1: Reflection and Gratitude

Take 10 minutes in the morning to reflect on the previous day. Jot down three things you're grateful for in your new role as a dad.

Day 2: Quality Time Inventory

Keep a log of your quality time with your baby and partner. You'll notice a pattern, which will help you add more quality time activities to your routine.

Day 3: Self-Care Check-In

Evaluate your self-care routine (yes, dads need self-care, too). Have you been getting enough sleep? Are you exercising? Are you getting time to do the things you love?

Day 4: Teamwork Evaluation

Have an open conversation with your partner about the first few days. Discuss what's working well, and evaluate areas for improvement. Brainstorm ways to share responsibilities and offer each other more support.

Day 5: Daddy and Baby Bonding Time

Plan a unique bonding activity with your baby. Take a photo or write a short description of the moment. It sounds cheesy, but trust me, you'll treasure the reminder.

Day 6: Sleep Quality Analysis

Keep a sleep journal detailing your baby's sleep patterns, as well as your own. This will help you figure out sleep strategies and feeding schedules.

Day 7: Proactive Changes

Based on your audit, list three proactive changes you want to make. They can be as small as reading a few pages of a novel before bed instead of scrolling on your phone.

Sleep Strategies for New Dads: Using Science to Hack Newborn Sleep

If you ask anyone about the newborn stage, they will probably mention sleep (or the lack of it). But you need to understand what "good" newborn sleep actually looks like so you can manage your expectations.

Steve mistakenly assumed that "sleeping like a baby" meant his daughter would be sleeping well in between feeds. What he hadn't considered was the time it took to change diapers and burp a baby, let alone soothe them back to sleep. But once he understood that his daughter considered two hours a solid sleep block, he adjusted his expectations and stopped feeling frustrated that he had a "bad sleeper."

Let's look at some baby sleep facts:

- Newborns usually sleep 14-17 hours every 24 hours, in two- to three-hour bursts.
- The parts of their brain that control day-night sleep haven't developed yet.
- Research shows that babies are twice as likely to wake up when touched during active sleep (which they spend most of their time in) (McNamara et al., 2002).

- Studies show that 20-30% of all infants experience night wakings for up to two years (Tham et al., 2017).

Baby Sleep Hacks

Like Steve, you need to have realistic expectations of your baby's sleep abilities. But that doesn't mean there aren't ways you can hack the process to get some extra shuteye.

#27 - Work With Their Internal Clock

Your baby's circadian rhythm revolves around food at this stage (kind of like when you were a teenager), but you can also help them learn more about a night-day system.

- Expose your baby to sunlight in the morning and the afternoon.
- Include daily activities that act as social cues, like a warm bath before bed.
- Have low-key evenings with dim lighting and no blue light.
- If your partner is pumping, be aware of pump times. Breast milk contains an amino acid called tryptophan, which is used to make melatonin (which, in turn, is super important for sleep). The levels of tryptophan in the milk are based on the mom's circadian rhythm. So, if your partner pumps your baby's milk in the morning, it can affect their melatonin levels and sleep.

#28 - Get Daytime Sleep Right

Your baby's day sleep and night sleep are intrinsically linked. Basically, your baby will sleep better at night when they nap better during the day. It's a tricky balance, because too much day sleep means less night sleep, but too little day sleep means an overtired baby.

Todd and Carrie had the sweetest baby during the day, because she slept most of the time. But at night, their little angel was wide awake. By 3:00 am, Todd and Carrie were exhausted and snapping at each other. Meanwhile, little Zoe was losing her cool, because she was overtired. Then, just as Todd and Carrie were at their breaking point, Zoe would fall asleep. After two weeks of adjusting their sleep strategies, Todd and Carrie finally found the day/night sweet spot.

- Research shows that when parents manage to lengthen waking time before bed, their babies need less help settling down and experience fewer sleep problems (Skúladóttir et al., 2005).
- Aim for a long lunch nap, because this is when your baby experiences a natural energy dip.
- Understand that developing any kind of baby sleep routine before four to six weeks is challenging. At this stage, babies are eating often and don't have the developmental tools to sleep better.
- Babywearing is an easy way to get longer daytime naps. In fact, a study found that three hours of babywearing reduced infant crying by 43% during the day and 54% at night (Increased Carrying Reduces Infant Crying: A Randomized Controlled Trial, 1986).

If you haven't already noticed, newborn sleep is erratic. But by 12 weeks, your baby is developmentally ready to start sleeping better (and by better, I mean four to five hours at a time). We will look at more sleep hacks in Chapter 3.

From a Woman's Perspective: Actionable, Practical Steps to Take

I'll never forget the moment we walked through the front door, our hearts bursting with equal parts joy and apprehension. Our baby, snug as a bug in their car seat, seemed so small and fragile in the grand scheme of things. And yet, as we crossed the threshold into our new reality, I knew that our lives would never be the same again.

The days that followed were a whirlwind of sleepless nights, diaper blowouts, and round-the-clock feedings. We stumbled through the chaos with a mixture of awe and exhaustion, marveling at the miracle of parenthood while simultaneously wondering if we were cut out for this whole parenting gig.

But I feel it's crucial to mention that some moms don't feel bonded with their babies immediately. You hear stories about parents who look at their new babies and feel an overwhelming rush of love, but that isn't the case for everyone. Sometimes, that bond grows slowly over time.

Be gentle: Your partner is hormonal and overwhelmed. Her body feels foreign and is constantly leaking. She is going through a metamorphosis, and the experience can be challenging.

- **Action steps:** Have nourishing and comforting meals planned for the first few weeks. You can have them in the freezer, get them delivered, or ask friends and family to help. Take over baby duty and give her time to shower or bathe and put on clean clothes. Make the bed and tidy the house so she doesn't feel overwhelmed.

Step up and step in: Your partner might not ask for help, but she shouldn't have to. Anticipate her needs as much as possible.

- **Action steps:** If she had a C-section, help with diaper changes and basic household chores while she heals. Your goal in those early weeks is to be hands-on in whatever way you can. A benefit of you helping out is that you get loads of bonding time with your baby while your partner looks after herself.

Key Takeaways

- Keep your baby's world small. Give yourself time to find your dad groove.
- Set clear boundaries with family and friends.
- Prioritize postpartum care.
- Find your feeding rhythm.
- Make sleep hygiene a priority to catch those much-needed Zzzs.
- Step up in the diapering department with a stocked diaper bag and changing table.
- Try out different techniques to calm your fussy baby.
- Do a New Dad Audit to help you get on top of time management and balance life with your new role.
- Come to terms with the fact that newborns eat often, which means broken sleep. But remember that those early weeks pass quicker than you think, and soon your baby will be sleeping for longer stretches.

Chapter Two
GROWTH SPURTS AND GRINS: THE PLAYBOOK FOR DAD'S NEXT CHAPTER (MONTHS 2-3)

"One of the greatest titles in the world is parent, and one of the biggest blessings in the world is to be one."
— *Jim DeMint*

You're officially in the trenches of fatherhood's second and third months. Buckle up, because you're in for a wild ride!

Remember those sleepless nights you thought would never end? Well, good news—they're starting to feel a little less like a scene from a horror movie and a little more like a bad dream you'll eventually wake up from. Sure, you're still stumbling through the dark like a zombie, but at least you've mastered the art of changing a diaper in record time.

From growth spurts and sleep regressions to fussiness and diaper blowouts, you'll quickly learn that nothing can fully prepare you for the rollercoaster ride that is fatherhood.

But even on the toughest days, when you feel like you're barely keeping your head above water, remember that you're doing an amazing job. Your baby may not be able to say it yet, but trust me, they're grateful for every cuddle, every kiss, and every sleep-deprived nighttime feed.

You should be proud of yourself for knuckling through the uncertainty and sleeplessness of the past few weeks. Fatherhood is an exhilarating change, but you're one month in, and there is so much adventure ahead of you.

Months Two and Three: What You Need to Know

Nothing makes you feel like a proud dad more than watching your baby do new things. But don't be militant about milestones. Your baby is unique, and you can likely already see their individual temperament developing. That means they'll hit milestones on their own personal timeline.

Memorable Milestones

- **Smiling!** Your baby may start smiling at you, and believe me, you won't care if it's still the "wind" smile of the first four weeks.
- **Your baby is starting to understand that certain voices go with particular faces.** You may notice that they coo or babble when you make facial expressions and interact with them. I'm sure you never thought you would be the type to get in touch with your inner baby, but watching your child get excited by your actions is priceless. It is worth all the baby talk and kooky faces.
- Your baby may be fascinated by your partner's dangly earrings (these will need to go soon). **Babies at this age can focus on objects and follow them with their eyes.** Your baby may even take a swipe at dangling objects, although their aim and grip aren't enough to do major earlobe damage, yet.
- **Your baby's neck is getting stronger**, which is fantastic news if you felt nervous handling your bobblehead newborn. They may be able to lift their head and torso up slightly on their arms. As you reach the three-month mark, your baby may even roll from their tummy onto their back.
- **Baby fussiness tends to peak between six and eight weeks.** After that, crying gets easier to deal with because there is usually a reason for the meltdown.

Two-Month Check-Up

Your baby will have several check-ups over the next year, starting at two months. Consider these appointments a trial run for future social outings. You can practice packing the diaper bag and working out the best backseat soothing techniques.

This check-up isn't anything to stress about. Your health care provider wants to know about eating, sleeping, and pooping—pretty much your life up to this point.

- They will take your baby's weight, length, and head circumference to check if they are growing according to schedule.
- Be prepared to answer feeding questions, like how often they feed. At this stage, your baby might make it longer between feeding sessions, eating eight times in 24 hours.
- Poop is also on the list. Your provider will want to know if you are changing several wet diapers and a few soft poops each day.
- Your baby can probably stay awake slightly longer during the day, and you may get questions about how long they sleep.
- Your baby may have vaccinations, depending on the schedule your health care provider uses.

This check-up is the perfect time for you to ask any questions you might have. As I sat in the pediatrician's office for our baby's two-month checkup, I had a list of questions longer than a CVS receipt. From the intricacies of baby poop to the mysteries of infant sleep, I was determined to leave no stone unturned.

But as I launched into my interrogation, our baby decided to chime in with a perfectly timed pooplosion that rivaled a volcanic eruption. As I frantically juggled diapers and wipes, I couldn't help but chuckle at how accurately the situation described parenthood. It's a learn-through-experience kind of gig.

In the end, I may not have gotten all the answers I was looking for, but I did learn one valuable lesson: Sometimes, the best way to navigate parenthood is with a healthy dose of humor and a whole lot of baby wipes.

Get Your Bonding On

Humor is a parenting superpower, and can also help you bond with your baby. Your baby is turning into a little person who thinks you're wonderful, but that doesn't mean they won't drive you mad sometimes. Your face and voice are some of their favorite things, and you probably can't get enough of that intoxicating baby smell (a good thing on those sleepless nights).

Your baby is curious about the world, and now is the perfect time to up your bonding game.

Talk: Chat to your baby about your day, or walk outside, explaining what you see. Not only will they respond to your voice, but talking with them helps you deepen your connection. Reading to your baby is another great option. I read Harry Potter to my daughter and loved every minute of it.

#29 - Try something called Parentese. This is a simple language and grammar spoken in a tone that engages your baby. You've probably been doing it already without realizing it. It's the high-pitched, sing-song voice you use when you talk to cute babies, including your own. Be sure to get up close and add big facial expressions into the mix.

#30 - Sportscasting is another fun technique that helps you chat with your baby. Think of yourself as a sports commentator. Tell your baby what's going on around them and what you are doing with them. For example, "I can see that you've wriggled out of your swaddle. Daddy needs to practice bundling you up. I'm tightening your swaddle so you feel snug and cozy."

Babywearing: Your baby may be awake for an hour to an hour and a half at a time throughout the day. That means it can be trickier to get things done. An easy fix is to pop them into a carrier. You can include them in daily activities, and you'll be surprised at how many small, precious interactions you have.

Dance and sing: Have fun with your baby. Pull out those dusty dance moves and bring the singing out of the shower. Parenthood requires a certain level of silliness, so start practicing early. Dancing and singing are also super effective options when you have a fussy baby.

The Feeding/Sleeping Train

You've probably spent the past few weeks of fatherhood figuring out eating and sleeping, but I have news for you: Balancing your baby's nutritional needs with their evolving sleep patterns is a full-time job. Plus, each baby is different and develops according to their own unique schedule.

Most babies at this stage eat 4-5 oz every three to four hours. That means six to eight feedings in between naps and nighttime sleeping. You're still following your baby's hunger cues and practicing demand-feeding, but that doesn't mean you can't start working on a schedule.

Helpful Hacks

#31 - **Day-night differentiation:** I'm sure you're desperate for long, uninterrupted nights, but your baby doesn't know the difference between night and day yet. You can help them get the message by making daytime feeds interactive, but keeping nighttime feeds quiet and low-stimulus.

#32 - **Cluster feeds:** Your goal is probably to get as many extra Zzz's as possible, and cluster feeds might be your best bet. A cluster feed is a series of quick feeds in a short space of time, usually in the evening. Cluster feeds can help keep your baby's tummy fuller for longer and score you some extra sleep.

#33 - **Morning wake-up:** Try to wake your baby up at the same time every morning. Work with their natural rhythm, and don't overthink it. My daughter would wake up between 7:00 and 7:30 a.m. and be down for a nap by 8:30 or 9:00 a.m. Having a similar wake-up time helped us get her into a daytime nap and feeding rhythm. Your baby probably sleeps 9-12 hours each night and 4-6 hours during the day. That could mean four to five naps a day. Remember, your baby can't self-soothe at this stage, and needs you to help them fall asleep or get back to sleep. Naps are usually short and erratic. If you've ever seen those memes of parents putting their sleeping babies into the crib like they're handling a bomb, that pretty much sums it up.

#34 - **Eat, play, sleep…or something like that:** Some experts say your baby should eat when they wake up, play, then nap again. This routine helps them fall asleep without a sleep association like a feed or rocking. But the eat, play, sleep routine isn't set in stone. Flora and I used a play, eat, and sleep scheme instead. We found our kids were the most responsive just as they woke up, and having a feed before a nap helped them sleep longer.

Tackling Common Challenges: Gas, Colic, Sleep Regressions, and Growth Spurts

Each stage of fatherhood comes with challenges, but the beauty of your journey is that you're learning and growing with your baby and your partner. No one has it all figured out. We're all going on instinct and gleaning tidbits of wisdom from other dads who are farther along the road than us.

The two- to three-month stage does have a few hurdles, but if you keep running and doing your best to scale them, you're winning.

Gas

As a new dad, I thought I was prepared for anything—spit-up, diaper blowouts, you name it—but nothing could have prepared me for the unrelenting force of nature that is a gassy baby.

It all started innocently enough, with a few cute little toots here and there. But as our baby's digestive system kicked into high gear, those innocent toots quickly escalated into full-blown explosions that could clear a room faster than a fire alarm.

At first, I tried to play it cool, laughing off the occasional fart like it was no big deal. But as the days turned into weeks, I found myself waging a losing battle against the relentless onslaught of baby gas.

From late-night burping sessions that resembled something out of a WWE match to desperate attempts at bicycle kicks that would put a Tour de France cyclist to shame, I tried every trick in the book to soothe our gassy little one—with varying degrees of success.

But amidst the chaos and occasional olfactory assault, there was the sweet relief of a well-timed burp or a perfectly executed gas pass. As any seasoned parent will tell you, there's nothing quite as satisfying as watching your baby let out a big, gassy sigh of relief after a particularly rough bout of gas.

Gas Tips:

#35 - Hold your baby's legs together, bend the knees slightly, and move their legs in a circular motion. This can help those pesky air bubbles work their way out.

#36 - While they are lying on their back, try gently stretching your baby's legs down. Then, gently push them up towards their tummy. This move almost always had our babies farting up a storm.

#37 - Move your baby's legs as if they were riding a bicycle.

#38 - Lay your baby on your arm, face down. Their tummy will be along your forearm and their head will be in your hand.

#39 - Try tummy time. Lying on their tummy can help get rid of gas, but be prepared for some spit-up.

Colic

Colic is the worst. If you have a colicky baby, I really am sorry. It can be demoralizing to listen to your baby cry inconsolably, but I'm also here to tell you that it will eventually be okay. It's a difficult season, but your baby will grow out of it.

My friend Jason was almost in tears while talking to me over coffee. His son had colic, and after four weeks, he was desperate. By this stage, his wife was crying as much as their baby, and he didn't know how to help either of them.

Understanding colic is tricky. It may be caused by allergies, gastroesophageal reflux disease, muscle tension, or an upset tummy. But many doctors will tell you that it could also just be how your baby is wired, and it's not your fault.

Let's look at the science around colic:

- Some studies have found that colic symptoms improved when the parents stimulated their babies less. There seems to be a link between colic symptoms and how the baby's brain processes information (Lucassen et al., 1998).
- Another study showed that colicky babies were slower to develop mature melatonin production rhythms, which could

explain why they're inconsolable when trying to wind down at night (İnce et al., 2018).

Use the Rule of Three if you're unsure whether your baby's crying is normal or colic. If your baby cries more than three hours per day at least three days a week for over three weeks, colic could be the culprit.

Colic Tips

#40 - My friend Justin said that a baby sling was the only thing that saved his sanity when his son had colic. He found that his son was calmer and would nap when his sore tummy was pressed to the warmth of his dad.

#41 - A pacifier can also be a great soothing tool for a distraught tot.

#42 - My sister swore by wrapping her son in a toweling diaper and putting him in a warm bath. The weight of the wet fabric and the warm water helped calm him when nothing else would.

Colic is a challenge, so remember to be patient with yourself and your partner. You are both probably running on minimal sleep, and your protective instincts fire up every time your baby screams. That means you're both working in high-stress mode. Be gentle with each other and tag-team baby duty. You'll each need a break.

Sleep Regression and Growth Spurt

If "sleep regression" isn't something you've heard parents complaining about, you're about to get your first taste. Some babies only have a sleep regression at around four months, but it's not unusual to experience it earlier. I want you to be prepared, so now seems the best time to bring it up.

It's not that your baby sleeps particularly well at this stage, but a sleep regression can make the little sleep they do have even worse.

Sleep regressions can be from:

- Growing pains
- Developmental milestones
- Changes in nap routine

Your baby may be restless and have trouble falling and staying asleep. That can make for one irritable little critter. Often, sleep regressions happen when your baby is about to learn a cool new skill. Different areas of the brain are linking and developing, and this internal shake-up means dicey sleep and a grumpy baby. Luckily, sleep regressions typically only last a few days to a week or two.

Your three-month-old may be launched into a sleep regression because of the three-month growth spurt. Around this time, your baby may wake up more at night to feed. They may also be especially cranky and hungry. That's because their body is growing like crazy. The onesie they wore today may literally not fit tomorrow! Your baby will quickly grow in length and gain weight, and that kind of sprouting can be uncomfortable. Let your baby eat and sleep as much as they want during this time. Try and stick to your regular routine if possible, but don't be married to it. These tricky times are about thriving, not just surviving, which means doing what works for you and your baby.

The Underrated Role of Dad Friends

I remember joining the guys at poker night and feeling so out of my element. These were some of my best friends, yet I felt disconnected from them. I didn't want the third beer, and couldn't follow the conversation because I was exhausted. Justin leaned over and said, "It gets easier." Later that night, he texted me the details of a dad's group he thought I might like.

That group was the lifeline I didn't know I needed. From swapping war stories about epic diaper blowouts to commiserating over the perils of sleep regression, the dad's group quickly became a sanctuary where I could vent, laugh, and find solace in the company of fellow dads who just "got it."

Perhaps the most valuable lesson I learned from my time in the dad's group wasn't about diaper-changing techniques or sleep-training methods—it was about the power of community and the profound impact that sharing our joys and struggles with others can have on our journey through parenthood.

Shifting Friendships

Understand that your friendship circle may shift now that you're a dad. You'll have less time for your friends in the early stages of parenthood, and your priorities will revolve around your new family. Being vulnerable with your friends might be hard, and they may get tired of you gushing over your baby's newfound rolling skills.

Fortunately, having a baby gives you access to an exclusive club—one filled with dads who get you. I'm not saying to close the chapter on your non-dad friends. They provide you with important space, freedom, and downtime that you need from dadhood. But I can't stress enough how impactful it can be to find a group of dads who are in the same boat as you.

Finding Your Brotherhood

Developing the right dad group creates a safe space for you to find practical advice and emotional support. Fatherhood is a lot, and you may be experiencing loneliness, isolation, and sleep deprivation. I know you love your baby, but that doesn't change the fact that they have turned your world upside down and cost way more than you expected. Dad stress is real.

You can find helpful parenting resources online, and even local directories for dad groups in your area. The group I joined met once a week, but also had a messaging forum. Late-night SOSs about projectile vomiting or midnight meetups with sleepless babies were common and offered us a sense of camaraderie and solidarity.

Don't be afraid to ask for help, and find the people who understand the wild ride of fatherhood.

Playtime

With your baby now staying awake slightly longer between naps, you finally get the chance to play with them. As a new dad, I quickly learned that playing with my baby was as much about bonding as it was about fun and games.

From the moment our little one entered the world, I made it my mission to become the master of playtime—armed with a repertoire of silly faces, funny noises, and tickle attacks that could rival a seasoned clown. Trust me, playing and spending time with your kids never gets old.

Use a mirror: Your baby will love looking at their own face, as well as yours while you make crazy facial expressions. The sillier, the better, so have fun with it.

High-contrast toys: According to Michigan State University, black-and-white patterns and images are easier for babies to focus on and can benefit vision development (Kylie Rymanowicz, Michigan State University Extension, 2014).

Gentle rattles: Soft rattles are easier for your baby to grasp. You can also use them for "tracking." Lay your baby on their back and hold the rattle in front of their face. Move it to the left and then right. Your baby should track the movement with their eyes. If they lose focus, give the rattle a shake to re-engage them.

Tummy time: A tummy time mat is cool, but you don't need to get fancy to do tummy time with your baby. Lie with them in front of a mirror or put a selection of interesting toys within their reach.

Dance: Flora and I danced with all our kids, and spontaneous kitchen dance parties are still a regular event in the King house. Moving up and down or side to side with your baby helps their vestibular system develop. This gives them an awareness of their body in space. Essentially, dancing with your baby can help them develop the skills they need to learn, self-regulate, and not fall off the play set at the park.

Play ideas are great, but what your baby really wants is time with you. Include them in your day, talk to them, and give them cuddles. Being a dad is a lot of things, but overcomplicated doesn't need to be one of them.

From a Woman's Perspective: Actionable, Practical Steps to Take

As a new mom, the first few months of motherhood felt like a whirlwind of emotions—from the overwhelming love and joy of welcoming our precious bundle into the world to the bone-deep exhaustion of sleepless nights and round-the-clock feedings.

Perhaps the most challenging part of those early months was navigating the rollercoaster ride of my own emotions—the highs of cuddling our baby close and marveling at their every coo and gurgle, and the lows of grappling with self-doubt and uncertainty about whether I was doing this whole motherhood thing right.

I thought things would have gotten easier by this point, but I was very wrong. My idea of motherhood was vastly different from my reality, and I struggled with my situation. In my head, motherhood looked like a Pinterest board. Idealistic and naive? Definitely.

No matter how many books I read, I was unprepared for cracked nipples, colic, and the disconnect I felt from my partner. I loved moments of motherhood, and that new baby smell makes everything better, but the journey would have been easier if my partner had understood where I was coming from and why those early months were such a contrast of emotions.

Listen: Sometimes, your partner just needs to vent. Unfortunately, telling people that motherhood wasn't what she expected often leads to judgment and gaslighting. You are the person she can open up to and feel safe with.

- **Action steps:** Learn about active listening and be the best damn sounding board you can. Your partner just needs empathy. If you can sneak a look at her Pinterest board, use it as inspiration. Maybe it's a cute post-baby maxi dress, newborn photos, or a more aesthetic nursery. Are there any visions of motherhood you can help bring to life?

Prioritize connection: A baby is demanding and takes up a lot of your time, but looking after your relationship is crucial, so you should take the initiative to connect.

- **Action steps:** Foot rubs, couch cuddles, or sharing a bubble bath are easy ways to add connection to your day. Sometimes, simple gestures like a good morning kiss or long hugs can give you both the connection you crave. Nothing cracks your heart wide open like seeing your partner with your baby, so sometimes it's as easy as spending time being together and playing with your bubs.

Key Takeaways

- Milestones are great, but they aren't the be-all and end-all. Your baby will develop on their own schedule, which could be a few weeks earlier or later than what the checklist says.
- Your 12-week check-up is the perfect time to ask questions.
- Creating a routine is a must. It will give you a solid base to work from as your baby's sleeping and eating patterns evolve.
- Colic is a major challenge. If none of the hacks I mentioned work, talk to your health care provider.
- Let your baby eat and sleep as much as they want during growth spurts (and buy some bigger onesies).
- Find a group that helps you be the best dad possible by providing a safe and supportive space.
- Don't overthink playtime. Just enjoy spending time with your baby.

Chapter Three
CRAWLING AND CUDDLES: A DAD'S GUIDE TO THE MOBILE MONTHS (MONTHS 4-6)

"Dads are most ordinary men turned into heroes, adventurers, storytellers, and singers of song."
— *Pam Brown*

Pat yourself on the back, Dad, and give your partner a kiss (or space, if she's feeling touched out). You survived the first three months. Hopefully, it was full of wonder, amazement, and love.

I'm sure there were challenging moments, but you did it! Your baby is now four months old and becoming more of a unique little human every day. They are probably pretty chunky, and you can finally handle them without worrying they'll break. In fact, you may even have experienced your first inadvertent punch to the face or head-butt.

Let's look at some of the exciting things the next few months hold for your dad journey.

Months Four to Six: What You Need To Know

Months four to six are packed full of dadtastic new adventures. Think pureed pumpkin and your baby's first mobile moments. You'll also have to contend with teething, and possibly sleep training, while navigating this next phase of parenthood with your partner.

Memorable Milestones

- Your baby will discover that tummy time is much more fun when they can roll around. **They will start rolling from their tummy onto their back**, and, in a few weeks, your little mover and shaker will also be rolling from their back to their tummy.
- This taste of freedom will soon have them **scooting or creeping on their belly** as they realize they can reach things they want.

- Not only can they reach things, but they can actually see them, too. **Your baby's visual range has increased.**
- **Your baby probably doesn't love strangers,** and may use their newfound self-expression to let you and the stranger at the supermarket know about it.
- After four months, **your baby can handle some solid food**—well, more like mush.
- By six months, your baby is probably **sitting without support** and keen to get crawling.

Teething Terror - Don't Worry, We've Got Tips

Teething is when your baby starts getting their first teeth. Unfortunately, it can be a pretty painful process for both kids and parents. Teething usually begins between four and seven months. The constant drool and fussiness can be frustrating, but knowing what to expect can help.

Your baby will probably get their two bottom front teeth first. Four to six weeks later, the upper two teeth will follow. By 11 months, your baby should have four teeth; by 15 months, they should have eight; by 19 months, they should have 12; and by 23 months, they should have 16.

But how do I know it's teething?

- Drooling (an excessive amount)
- Chewing and gnawing on everything (like a dog with a bone)
- Irritability (crankiness you can't explain)

- Rubbing their ears
- Sleep issues
- Flushed cheeks

Your baby's gum will also be red and swollen. You may even be able to feel the tooth if you rub the gum.

Teething is a process, and some babies handle it better than others. Here are some helpful tips to see you through the worst of teething.

#43 - The drool is real, so change their clothes regularly to prevent a rash. We had a million bibs on hand because it was easier to change a bib than an entire outfit.

#44 - Invest in some chew toys, preferably ones with texture. Chewing on something slightly rough will help with itchy gums.

#45 - Wet a washcloth and pop it into the freezer for a few minutes. Don't let it freeze solid, but let it get super cold. Chewing on a slightly frozen cloth ticks the texture box, and the cold helps soothe the gums.

#46 - Make frozen formula or breast milk popsicles.

Get Chatting - Communicating With Your Baby

It was one of those typical evenings in the life of a new dad—tired, slightly frazzled, but utterly in love. I cradled my baby in my arms, trying to decipher the meaning behind her coos and gurgles. "Alright kiddo, spill the beans," I joked, leaning in closer to her face. "What's on your mind tonight? Of course, her response was a bubbly string of baby babble. As I continued to chat with my little one, sharing stories about my day and asking for her input on life's pressing matters (like which onesie to wear tomorrow), I couldn't help but marvel at the beauty of our communication. It may have been simple and one-sided, but it was a connection, nonetheless.

At this stage, your baby is more engaged and interactive. They will even respond to their name. When they're awake, you're probably being bombarded with coos and babbles, but these sounds will become more intentional. "Bababa" and "mamama" are the order of the day. Practice taking turns talking with your baby. Respond when they interact with you, and then wait for them to respond. Not only does turn-taking mimic a real conversation, but your baby will make the cutest sounds and facial expressions.

Your baby might not be keen on strangers, but they're desperate to connect with you, so here are my pro tips.

#47 - Make and maintain eye contact.

#48 - Smile at your baby as often as possible.

#49 - Exaggerate your facial expressions. Your baby will try to mimic them, and this strengthens your bond.

At this stage, your baby is also more coordinated and will try to reach and grab things.

One sunny afternoon, while out for a stroll with my little one and Flora, I witnessed that coordination in action. As we walked, I noticed my baby's eyes light up with fascination as she reached out to grab something dangling from my wife's ear. Before I could react, her tiny fingers latched onto my wife's earring gave it an enthusiastic tug.

"Whoa there!" I exclaimed, trying to suppress a chuckle as I gently pried her hand away from the shiny bauble. "Looks like we've got ourselves an aspiring jewelry connoisseur."

From that moment on, I made a mental note to buy Flora studs for her birthday and find something shiny and dangly for our baby to play with.

I noticed my baby's interest and the excited leg kicking that happened when she grabbed that earring. Babies might not be able to talk yet, but they can still be super expressive.

Play Is Communication

From now until your child reaches adulthood, play will be a crucial part of their communication. They can't yet talk in a way you can understand, but playing gives you a glimpse into their world. It helps you relate to them, laugh with them, and enjoy them when the wild ride of parenthood feels like too much. So, why not practice playing and make it a part of your relationship?

Peek-a-Boo

Hide your face behind your hands or a blanket, then quickly reveal your face while saying "peek-a-boo!"

Pat-a-Cake

Sing the Pat-a-Cake nursery rhyme while clapping your hands in rhythm. You can also gently clap your baby's hands together.

I Spy

Hold up a colorful or interesting object within your baby's view and say, "I spy with my little eye something [color or description]." You can let your baby track the object with their eyes, or put it in front of them during tummy time.

Nursery Rhyme Singing

Sing nursery rhymes or lullabies to your baby, accompanied with simple actions. Use exaggerated facial expressions and different voices to keep your baby engaged.

Storytime with Picture Books

Read picture books to your baby, using funny voices and facial expressions. As a new dad, I quickly discovered the magic of reading aloud to our baby. With each turn of the page, I watched as their eyes widened with wonder, their tiny fingers reaching out to touch the colorful illustrations dancing across the pages. From classic fairy tales to silly rhymes and bedtime stories, our reading adventures became a cherished ritual.

Searching for Sleep - Is Sleep Training Right for You?

I'm sure you're hoping I'm going to tell you that your baby is about to start sleeping through the night…but I'm not. I'm going to be honest and say that struggling with sleep is normal, and that the phrase "sleeping like a baby" is grossly inaccurate. By four months, your baby is developmentally ready to start sleeping three hours or more in a row, but they'll still need to feed, so a solid eight hours of sleep is unrealistic.

If you're desperate and want to help your baby sleep better, you can try sleep training. Sleep training essentially teaches your baby to self-soothe so that they put themselves back to sleep when they wake up at night.

You may have heard horror stories of parents leaving their babies to scream in the hope that "crying it out" would get them to sleep. But many popular sleep training methods don't ask you to ignore your baby when they're upset.

Let's dive into some sleep training options, so you and your partner can decide which is best for your family.

Positive Routine With or Without Bedtime Fading

The idea behind a positive routine approach to sleep training is that babies will fall asleep more quickly if they have a set of predictable, enjoyable, quiet bedtime routines. Bedtime fading is a gentle "no cry" technique that can help your baby fall asleep more easily.

So, how does this actually work?

- Decide what to include in your bedtime routine. For Flora and me, it was a warm bath, a baby massage, and a feed.

- The trick is to only start the bedtime routine when your baby is drowsy, or you'll have a fight on your hands. If your baby is fighting sleep, they aren't tired enough.
- You'll need to pay close attention to your baby's sleep patterns and notice their natural bedtime. This could be 8:00 p.m. or later, depending on your baby.
- Once you know the usual time your baby goes to sleep, shift the bedtime earlier by 10-15 minutes every few days until you reach the bedtime you want.

Pro Tips

#50 - Assess your evening routine and cut out things like screen time and late naps that might keep your baby awake.

#51 - Stick with the same morning wake-up time, regardless of when your baby went to bed. This helps build up "sleep pressure" and will make them readier for bed at night.

#52 - Get morning sunlight on your baby's eyeballs. This helps regulate their circadian rhythm and gives their brain powerful sleep and awake time cues.

Extinction With Parental Presence

I know this sounds complicated, so let's break it down.

This method is also called the "chair method." The idea is that you put your baby in bed while they're awake and sit in a chair nearby until they fall asleep. Over time, you move the chair further away from their bed. You should do a quiet activity that seems boring to your child so they don't pay attention to you.

After a few successful nights, put your baby into bed and leave the room for a few seconds. The trick is to return before they start crying. This shows your baby they can be alone without freaking out. When your baby wakes up at night, wait one to three minutes before checking on them. This gives your baby the chance to self-soothe.

Some parents find this method difficult because they don't want to leave their baby to cry, even if it is only for a few minutes.

The "Pick Up, Put Down" Method

The goal of sleep training is to help your baby learn to self-soothe. If an extinction approach is a bit much for you, the "pick up, put down" method might be better.

This method involves staying in the room with your baby while they fall asleep independently. You put your baby into bed awake and give them the chance to self-soothe. If they cry, pick them up and comfort them before putting them back into bed, awake and calm.

This method can be tiring and time-consuming, but it might make you feel better about sleep training.

The Ferber Method

Probably the most controversial option, the Ferber method is also known as "crying it out." Parents put their babies to sleep without using rocking, feeding, or other soothing techniques. As the name suggests, parents then leave their babies to cry for progressively longer periods of time before checking on them.

Richard Ferber, who created this method, says that most kids are sleeping through by the third or fourth night. It's important to note that success depends on following the plan closely and consistently. This method should only be used with babies six months or older.

This method can be super stressful for parents. Hearing your baby crying and choosing to ignore them is too much for some parents. My friend Dylan shared with me that trying to sleep train their daughter using this method was one of the most stressful things ever. But, some of the men in my dad's group said that, although it was hard, pushing through was worth it.

Choosing the Right Option for You

I'm not here to tell you whether to sleep train your baby or not. Flora and I decided that positive routines were the best option for our family, but there is no right or wrong answer here. You all need sleep, and if sleep training will help you be the best, most well-rested parent you can be, then go for it. There are entire books about sleep training, and I've simply given you a short overview of the most popular methods. Do some research, chat with your partner, and decide on your next steps.

Starting Solids 101

Introducing your baby to solid food is a whole thing!

I was determined to make introducing solids to our baby a memorable and enjoyable experience. Armed with an array of pureed fruits and vegetables, I embarked on our culinary adventure with all the enthusiasm of a Michelin-star chef. From mashed bananas to pureed peas and everything in between, I pulled out all the stops in my quest to turn our baby into a gourmet connoisseur—with varying degrees of success (and by varying, I mean we were both wearing more food than eating it).

Although breast milk or formula will still be their primary food source for a while, solid food can be an exciting adventure.

According to the Dietary Guidelines for Americans and the American Academy of Pediatrics, babies should only have solid food at a minimum of four months, while six months is the more common age.

How do I know if my baby is ready to try solids?

- Your baby can sit up without support.
- They have good head and neck control.
- Your baby is interested in food (you may have noticed them eyeing your food).
- When you attempt solids the first few times, your baby swallows the food rather than pushing it out with their tongue.

But what do I feed them?

By seven months, your baby should be able to eat a variety of foods, including protein, fruits, vegetables, grains, yogurt, and cheeses. Cooked apples, bananas, butternut squash, and sweet potato are popular first food options.

Solid Food Tips

#53 - It's best to introduce one food at a time, with three to five days between options. This way, you can see if your child has any allergies. Cow milk, eggs, fish, shellfish, peanuts, and soy are common allergies.

#54 - Up until this point, your baby has only had liquid food, so they may struggle with different textures. Mash, puree, or strain food to make it smooth.

#55 - Let your baby get dirty. Put food on a tray and let them touch and feel it. Their fingers will inevitably end up in their mouths. Sometimes, we micromanage our baby's experiences instead of letting them be curious and explore.

#56 - Include iron-rich foods, like minced meat, chicken, fish, mashed eggs, and cooked legumes.

Foods to Avoid

- Anything your baby can choke on.
- No honey before 12 months.
- Undercooked eggs.
- Low-fat dairy.
- No dairy alternatives until two years old.

If introducing solids freaks you out, put it off for a few months. There is no rush. Watching your baby experience food for the first time should be exciting, so don't start until you're ready to enjoy the experience.

From a Woman's Perspective: Actionable, Practical Steps to Take

Navigating motherhood during months four to six can feel like finding your rhythm on a rollercoaster. You're learning to balance the ups and downs, finding moments of calm and stability amidst the chaos. You're discovering what works best for you and your baby, gradually settling into a routine that feels right for your family. It doesn't help that your baby is learning, growing, and constantly changing things up.

Here are some insights into how your partner may feel that can help you support and connect with her.

Accept your parenting differences: You're trying to figure out what works and what doesn't with your baby. Often, your methods will be different. That's fine, most of the time—but it is important to talk about it.

- **Action steps:** Listen to your partner's point of view when it comes to diaper brands, bottles, and nighttime feeds. It's important that you also help troubleshoot in challenging situations, and not just shift the mental load to your partner.

Re-evaluate household responsibilities: Equity is essential, and your partner will be able to focus on what really matters (your baby) when she feels supported and happy. Washing the dishes, doing laundry, and grocery shopping are just some of the things your partner might need help with if she is your baby's go-to.

- **Action steps:** See how you can make both your lives easier. Try a meal delivery service twice a week, or let your sister fold that load of laundry (you know, the one that lives on the sofa or the end of your bed). Your partner might not ask for help, but you should take it when friends and family offer.

Give her a break: Your partner may not say it (because mom guilt is real), but she needs a break from your baby. I remember going for a solo coffee and sandwich at our local garden center before buying a few herbs to plant at home. It was only 10 minutes from our house, so I was close enough to get home quickly, but far enough to feel free. That break was the relief I needed so I could refocus on our child without going crazy.

- **Action steps:** Take your baby for a walk or put them down for a nap so your partner can get out. The goal here isn't to free her up to do household chores—it's to give her space to breathe.

Couples experience this stage differently because each baby is unique. We had a baby who struggled with sleep, while my best friend's baby was sleeping five-hour stretches by four months of age. Your needs will be unique, so it's crucial that you talk with your partner to find out how best to support her.

Key Takeaways

- Your baby is more mobile and starting to explore the world around them. This is an exciting time, but you should check that your baby-proofing is up to snuff.
- Between teething and a fear of strangers, expect your baby to be clingy. Try to reframe clinginess. The fact that your baby turns to you for comfort and security means you're their safe space. It's a really good sign of secure attachment. Good job, Dad!
- Teething is tricky, but it does pass. Invest in some chew toys and bibs and embrace the journey.
- You model communication for your baby, so start chatting. Be expressive, use different tones, and smile at them.
- Millions of parents struggle with sleep, so you're not alone. Sleep training is an option at this stage if it's something you and your partner want to try.
- Starting solid food is an exciting experience for the whole family. Your baby gets to experience different tastes and textures, and you can enjoy watching them explore. If starting solids freaks you out, chat with your pediatrician for some tips.

Chapter Four

LITTLE EXPLORER, BIG DISCOVERIES: NAVIGATING THE SEVEN-TO NINE-MONTH ADVENTURE IN DADHOOD (MONTHS 7-9)

"Fathering is not something perfect men do, but something that perfects the man."

— *Frank Pittman*

During months seven to nine, your little one is like an intrepid explorer, eagerly discovering the world around them. From crawling and cruising to grabbing and tasting everything in sight, every day is a new adventure filled with wonder and curiosity. It's certainly a time that keeps you on your toes.

Months Seven to Nine: What You Need to Know

There are some exciting milestones during the next three months, as your baby starts crawling and exploring the world around them. While you're basking in the joys of parenthood, sleep can still be a bit elusive during months seven to nine. Your baby may experience sleep regressions or disruptions due to teething, growth spurts, or developmental milestones, but you and your partner will find ways to adapt and overcome the challenges together.

Memorable Milestones

- **Crawling is a major milestone.** You may see your baby doing the army crawl, the crab crawl, or even the backward crawl.
- **Your baby will start pulling up on furniture.** Now, nothing within reach is safe!
- **Their hand-eye coordination is much better**, so they can grab your car keys off the coffee table and make for the hills.
- **Object permanence** means your baby now understands that things exist even if they can't see them.
- **Your baby will learn about cause and effect**, thanks in part to their ability to pull things off surfaces.

- **Stranger anxiety** and clinginess reach a peak over the next few months.
- You may notice your baby picking up food with their thumb and forefinger. This is the **pincer grasp,** and an important developmental milestone.

#57 - Being the cool dad that you are, you've probably already babyproofed your home. But now that your little critter is on the move, you should double-check outlets, cabinet latches, and any places that might need taller baby gates.

Your Unique Baby

Your baby has always been unique, but you may be seeing more of their temperament emerge as they start to explore. We have three kids, and they couldn't be more different. Their incredible and unique characters have made parenting a pretty wild adventure, and certainly kept us on our toes.

Understanding your baby's temperament can help you parent the child you have, not the child you wish you had. What does that mean, exactly? Well, our firstborn was quiet and "good" as far as babies go. Our second-born, however, had very strong opinions about how he wanted to do things. Flora and I had to learn how to deal with each of our kids based on who they were, not who we wanted them to be.

Your baby's temperament will include specific characteristics and impact their response to their environment.

For example, they may be

- Sensitive to certain textures
- Shy
- Persistent
- Stubborn
- Busy

Understanding what makes your baby tick will be a massive help when you're creating routines, venturing outside the house, and trying to bond with them.

Your Mobile Baby's Motor Skills

Once your baby has the basics of crawling down, there's no stopping them. Their curiosity will have them zooming around the house, trying to get into and onto everything in sight. Your heart might need a minute to adjust, but this exploration is crucial for their development. The more your baby explores, the more capable they become, which means less accidents.

Here are some pro-dad hacks to help with motor development.

#58 - **Make an obstacle course:** Use the sofa, cushions, and blankets to create a challenging (but soft) adventure course for your baby. They will love crawling over and under things, and it will help them develop balance and confidence.

#59 - **Use a Pickler Triangle:** A Pickler Triangle is a wooden climbing frame that helps babies develop balance, muscle growth, coordination, and confidence.

#60 - **Sensory experiences:** Getting outside with your baby is the best sensory experience they can have. If you can't get outside, make a sensory bin. Sensory play helps develop the fine motor skills they will need for tying their laces or zipping up their coat.

What should go in a sensory bin? Almost anything! Textured toys, spaghetti, water, lentils, sand, sticks, you name it.

#61 - **Look at the nursery space:** Make the nursery a fun, safe play space:

- Choose furniture with rounded edges and soft corners.
- Keep toys and play materials within easy reach.
- Rotate toys regularly to keep your baby engaged and interested in exploring new textures, colors, and shapes.

Bonding Through Play: Encouraging Exploration and Curiosity

We've already seen that play is part of how your baby communicates. But now, playing is way more fun, because your baby is much more interactive.

Play is vital because it builds your baby's brain. Problem-solving, cause and effect, decision-making, emotional regulation, and social skills happen during play. Sensory play, in particular, helps develop neural connections.

Here are my top tips for playing with your baby at this stage:

#62 - Create a safe environment: When the space is safe, you can spend more time engaged with your baby and less time worrying about them.

#63 - Use toys: Blocks, shape and size sorters, and sensory board books were absolute winners in our house.

#64 - Real-life items: If you haven't already noticed, your baby is probably more interested in the TV remote or car keys than the developmentally appropriate toys you spent tons of money on. Welcome to parenthood! My advice is to have a basket filled with household items your baby can play with. Think wooden spoons, Tupperware, measuring cups, pots, a whisk, old remotes (batteries removed), and boxes.

#65 - Get outside: Some of the best advice I ever got was to go outside when our baby was driving us nuts. Sometimes, we just let them crawl around and explore. Other times, we would let them play with water or mud.

#66 - Rotate toys: This is a game-changer. Have baskets of toys or household items that you swap out weekly. That way, your baby has enough time to play with the items before the novelty wears off.

#67 - Follow your baby's lead: Pay attention to your baby's cues and interests during playtime.

#68 - Be present and engaged: Avoid distractions like phones or screens, and enjoy spending time with your baby. They're pretty quick at this stage, and you'll need to be at the top of your game, anyway.

#69 - Keep it simple and fun: You don't need fancy toys or elaborate setups to play with your baby. Let your creativity and imagination guide you as you explore new ways to play together.

#70 - Embrace the mess and chaos: Playtime can be messy, noisy, and chaotic, and that's okay! Embrace the mess and chaos as part of the fun, and focus on the joy and laughter shared with your baby.

Your Developing Baby Needs Routine

As a dad who made it through the baby stage and is now contending with tweens, I can't overemphasize how important routines are. They are the backbone of a successful home life (and your sanity).

Predictability and security: Babies thrive on consistency and predictability. A consistent routine helps them know what to expect throughout the day, giving them a sense of security and stability.

Regulated sleep patterns: A structured routine with consistent nap times and bedtimes can help regulate your baby's sleep patterns. That means longer sleep sessions, both during the day and at night. What a winner!

Top Tips for a Rad Routine

#71 - Establish a consistent wake-up time for your baby each morning.

#72 - Pay attention to your baby's natural sleep cues and establish consistent nap times. Aim for two to three naps per day, spaced evenly throughout the day.

#73 - Introduce regular meal times for breakfast, lunch, and dinner, along with scheduled breastfeeding or bottle-feeding sessions.

#74 - Have a calming bedtime routine to signal to your baby that it's time to wind down and prepare for sleep.

Of course, life happens, so here are some hacks to keep you on track when life goes awry.

#75 - Stick to the core elements of your routine, like a consistent wake-up and bedtime, but be flexible in the middle bits.

#76 - Make space for moments of play, exploration, and bonding. A routine helps guide your day, but it shouldn't dictate it.

#77 - Stay calm. Your baby can pick up on your emotions, so freaking out because the day has gone to hell will only make it worse.

Pesky Problems at Seven to Nine Months

As you've probably noticed, each stage of parenthood comes with challenges. The good news is that you keep adding tips and skills to your parenting toolbox, ready to whip them out when you need them.

Sleep Struggles

If sleep is still a fleeting hope in your life, I understand the frustration and sense of resignation you're probably feeling. Your baby has been tearing through developmental milestones lately, but with that comes sleep regressions and messed-up schedules. I feel like baby sleep is something parents never quite figure out, so don't feel bad.

At this stage, your baby probably sleeps 12-14 hours daily—9-12 hours at night (not in a row, unfortunately) and two to three hours during the day. They might still need one or two feeds at night, or they could just be waking up for comfort.

#78 - Try to comfort your baby first before offering them a feed. If they go back to sleep easily, you know that they aren't hungry and you can work on encouraging longer stretches of sleep.

The trick is not to let them sleep too much during the day, but also not to let them get overtired. There's a fine line between the two, so you'll need to watch your baby's sleep cues carefully to find the right balance.

Separation Anxiety

Separation anxiety can be super stressful for both you and your baby. There's nothing worse than having to leave your child when they're upset, but I wasn't prepared for my baby screaming blue murder when I walked out of the room for two minutes. Cut to me trying to do my bathroom business holding a screaming baby, with a curious toddler peeping around the door.

Babies at this stage are more aware of their surroundings and have developed a strong attachment to their parents. But that means they lose their secure base and sense of safety when you leave the room. Your baby can't understand the concept of time yet. Can you imagine how scary that must be? They know you've left, but have no idea when you'll be back. It makes sense that they would cry and cling to you.

Separation anxiety sucks, but here are some tried and tested hacks to help:

#79 - **Keep transitions short:** Long, drawn-out goodbyes only make the situation worse. Have a goodbye ritual that helps your baby transition, and then get out of there.

#80 - **Gradual separation:** Ease your baby into separations by gradually increasing the time apart.

#81 - **Tick all the boxes:** Make sure your baby isn't tired, hungry, or feeling sick.

#82 - **Encourage independence:** Let your baby explore so they feel confident in being away from you.

#83 - **Have a comfort object:** Can I tell you a secret? Flora still has her "lovey" in a box at the bottom of the cupboard. If your baby has a comfort object like a stuffed toy or blanket, it gives them a sense of comfort and security when they're away from you.

Separation anxiety can also happen at night, which might explain why your baby keeps waking up. Although it's frustrating, separation anxiety is temporary, and it will pass.

From a Woman's Perspective: Actionable, Practical Steps to Take

Wow, this stage is busy! Your baby is on the move, causing chaos and giving you heart failure in the process. I noticed that my kids always wanted to be where I was. They were constantly underfoot or trying to climb up my leg. This made cooking dinner or hanging out the laundry a real adventure.

Something I wasn't prepared for was the fact that separation anxiety seemed to apply to me more than Maddox. Saying goodbye to Dad wasn't nearly as dramatic as my exit. So, dads, keep in mind that your partner may have more guilt and anxiety about leaving your baby.

Run baby interference: If your partner is getting dressed, cooking dinner, or using the toilet, distract your baby. Simple tasks are 10 times harder with a cute critter climbing up your leg.

- **Action steps:** Plan playtime or put your baby down for a nap when your partner needs to get stuff done. Trust me, she'll appreciate the chance to poop in peace.

Show appreciation and affection: Your partner might feel a bit lost in her new mom role. She's spending all of her energy caring for those around her, but is probably a bit burned out and overwhelmed.

- **Action steps:** Show your partner you love, respect, and appreciate her. Before giving her a hug, ask her if she's touched out. Having a baby constantly touching you can make you extremely sensitive to physical touch, and she's liable to freak out if you try anything without checking first.

Take over nighttime duties: Volunteer to take on nighttime responsibilities, such as soothing the baby back to sleep or handling diaper changes. This gives your partner a real baby break.

- **Action steps:** Prep bottles, and even sleep in another room with your baby or the baby monitor so Mom can enjoy uninterrupted, guilt-free rest.

Key Takeaways

- Prepare to be busy as your baby starts crawling and exploring the world around them.
- Don't be afraid to let them get dirty, because the best learning happens through sensory play.
- Focus on parenting the baby you have, not the baby you hoped for (like one who actually sleeps).
- Find a routine and rhythm that works for your family.
- Separation anxiety is hard, but it's not forever.

Chapter Five

BRIDGING THE BABY GAP: MASTERING MILESTONES IN THE LAST LAP OF YEAR ONE (MONTHS 10-12)

"[My father] always provided me a safe place to land and a hard place from which to launch."

— *Chelsea Clinton*

Can you believe it? You've officially reached the final chapter of your baby's first year—and toddlerhood is looming. From those unforgettable first moments in the delivery room to the countless cuddles, giggles, and milestones along the way, you've experienced the full spectrum of parenthood in just 10 short months, but there's so much more to come.

As a dad, reaching the last two months of my baby's first year felt like standing on the peak of a mountain after a long and crazy climb. It was a bittersweet moment, filled with a whirlwind of emotions as I reflected on the incredible journey we'd been on together. Books, classes, and advice can get you to base camp, but reaching that final peak is all about hands-on learning and trust.

Months 10-12: What You Need to Know

These last few months are a time of monumental growth, unforgettable moments, and a touch of nostalgia as you prepare to bid farewell to the baby stage and welcome your little one into toddlerhood. Not only has your baby been going through big changes, but so have you.

Memorable Milestones

- **Your baby is cruising—literally.** They'll be holding onto furniture and moving around. They may even try to take their first independent steps.
- If you've been anxiously waiting for that **magical first word**, you're in luck. Keep your ears open and cross your fingers that it's "Daddy."

- **Fine motor skills are also moving along nicely,** and your not-so-little baby can probably turn the pages of a book and stack blocks.
- Your mini-me is already proving they're a force to be reckoned with as they test out their **problem-solving abilities.**

Responsive Parenting - Your Best Defense Against Toddler Terror

If you haven't already noticed, your baby is growing into a unique and quirky character that pushes boundaries and tests limits. The next few months will see your baby transition into toddlerhood, which is a pretty special time.

I remember chatting with my friend Justin as he neared the end of his first year of fatherhood, and his words really struck me. He said, "I didn't feel like a real parent until now." I was pretty confused and asked him to explain. "Up until this point, I've been focused on keeping my baby alive. But now, he has an opinion about everything. I'm realizing there's a whole other dimension to being a dad that has more to do with raising a good person than taking care of the basics."

Truth.

Having a baby and being a parent are very different things, and this stage of development makes that very clear.

You've probably heard that the toddler years are hellish, but I don't think they have to be. Responsive parenting is essentially a continuation of what you've been doing. You notice your child's cues, figure out what they need, and respond to them. This gets trickier when your small human is having a meltdown in the store, but being emotionally present while holding firm to your boundaries is exactly what your little tyrant needs.

Raising Trailblazers: The Art of Empowering Autonomy in Tiny Tots

If your baby hasn't started making demands yet, it's coming. But this newfound push for independence is good, and you should embrace it. I know you're worried they'll hurt themselves, but freedom actually makes them safer. The more confident your baby is, the more skills they develop.

Handing your child more control can feel scary, but with the right strategies, you can help equip your baby with the skills they need to run the world.

Offer choices: Allow your almost-toddler to make simple choices throughout the day, such as what clothes to wear, which toy to play with, or what snack to have out of the options you give them.

Encourage independence: Your baby is more capable than you know, so let them do things for themselves, like get dressed or feed themselves.

Foster problem-solving skills: Encourage your toddler to independently solve problems and overcome challenges. You don't want to be a "curling" parent. Curling is a sport where players use brooms to sweep the ice in front of a sliding stone, guiding its path and reducing friction. A curling parent makes things too easy for their baby.

Set realistic expectations: Give your baby age-appropriate tasks. You can ask them to find all the socks while folding laundry, or to pack away toys. Praise the process, not the outcome, because this makes your baby feel valued and empowered.

Playtime Pioneers: Unleashing Your Inner Kid for Baby's Development

Garth wasn't convinced that playing was for him. Although his baby was cute, the repetitive baby talk and exaggerated facial expressions could get a bit boring. But as his baby grew and developed, things started to shift for him. As time passed, he realized that the true magic of playtime wasn't in the toys or activities—it was in the connection he shared with his baby. As they laughed, bonded, and explored the world through imagination, he felt overwhelming joy and gratitude for the precious moments they were creating together.

Playing with your baby helps their language development and motor skills. Plus, it gets more fun as your baby's personality shines through. But if playing is still a struggle, here are some top game ideas from my super helpful dad's group that helped them become pros.

Storytelling adventures: Your baby won't care how random your stories are, so have fun with it. The sillier the stories are, the better. Use descriptive language, sound effects, and expressive gestures to bring the story to life and engage your toddler's imagination.

Rhyme time sing-along: Sing and clap, and encourage your toddler to join in by singing, clapping, and moving to the rhythm.

Your hand gestures and facial expressions can help them understand concepts and words. YouTube is your best friend here.

Labeling and sorting game: Play doesn't need to be fancy. Keep it simple with things you can find around the house. Encourage your toddler to identify and label each item by name, using simple words and phrases. You can also sort the objects into categories based on color, shape, size, or function. Be descriptive about each item, including what they do and how you use them.

Puzzle playtime: Puzzles are a fantastic play and learning tool. Start with simple wooden or foam puzzles with large, easy-to-grasp pieces. Puzzles help develop problem-solving skills, hand-eye coordination, and spatial awareness.

Shape-sorting fun: If you're looking for something to keep your baby busy, show them how to match containers with their lids. Your Tupperware cupboard will never look better.

DIY ball ramp: Did you ever have a marble run as a kid? Make a bigger version using cardboard tubes, paper towel rolls, or PVC pipes. You'll be surprised how long this keeps your baby busy.

Dad and Me: Moments of Magic with Your 10- to 12-Month-Old

As I fumble with the coffee maker, trying to coax it into action with my still-half-asleep brain, I hear a familiar sound from the living room—the unmistakable squawk of my baby's favorite toy, the singing duck.

With a sigh, I abandon my quest for caffeine and head into the living room, where I find my baby gleefully pressing the button on the singing duck over and over again, each press eliciting another round of off-key quacking.

"Ah, the joys of parenthood," I mutter to myself, mustering a tired smile as I join in the chorus of quacks, much to my baby's delight.

But as I sit there, surrounded by the chaos of breakfast crumbs and squeaky toys, I can't help but marvel at the bond I share with my child. In that moment, as we laugh and quack together, I realize that these simple, silly moments make all the sleepless nights and diaper disasters worth it.

At the end of the day, it's not about having all the answers or doing everything perfectly—it's about forging a bond with your baby that's built on love, laughter, and a shared appreciation for the finer things in life, like singing ducks and morning coffee.

Here are my top three bonding hacks to help you be the super dad you want to be:

#84 - **Get down on their level.** You know that feeling of intimidation you get when standing next to a much bigger guy? Well, consider what it's like for your baby to look up at you from the ground. Bend down or sit with them when you interact. Your baby will love the connection, and you'll fend off the inevitable clicks and cracks of aging knees.

#85 - **Get ready to rumble.** Bring out your best WWE moves, because rough-and-tumble play is where it's at. Dads play differently than moms, and it's crucial for your baby's brain.

Rough-and-tumble play has been linked to reduced aggression and increased self-regulation in kids (Freeman & Robinson, 2022). Have you ever thrown your baby up in the air or had an impromptu wrestling match? That kind of play helps your baby assess risk and test their limits.

#86 - **Get creative (and silly).** Imaginative play is where the magic happens. Don't be afraid to dress up, have tea parties, or go on a dinosaur adventure in the garden.

Ready, Set, Toddler! Getting Set for the Exciting Transition from Babyhood

Heading into toddlerhood means getting to know a new little person. Over the last few months, your baby has been enjoying their newfound taste for independence, but now they have the physical skills to back it up. It can be an interesting combination that will keep you on your toes.

Your baby is starting to develop preferences for food, clothes, toys, and how they like their toast cut in the morning. It's a whole new side to parenting, and I'm here to help you navigate it with confidence.

Exploring New Tastes: Diving into a World of Varied and Textured Diets

By this stage, your baby is having three meals a day and in a transitional phase of their eating journey. Now that they have a couple of teeth, you can get more creative in the kitchen. The more flavors you introduce early on, the more adventurous an eater you're likely to have.

One of the easiest ways to tempt your little critter to munch on new things is to eat the rainbow and create fun flavor and texture combos.

Make meals colorful with things like:

- Peas, asparagus, zucchini
- Sweet potato, carrot
- Banana, pineapple
- Blueberries
- Raspberries, tomatoes, red pepper

Include grains like:

- Cooked noodles
- Bread
- Rice
- Couscous

Protein is also a must, so add:

- Eggs, chicken, beef, fish
- Beans, nut butter

Alec found that the easiest way to coax his twins to eat was to make snack platters of finger foods. Julienned carrots, cheesy omelet squares, and mini-waffles with berries were some of his go-to options. Tom liked to use scrambled eggs as a base for vegetables and oatmeal for stewed fruit and berries.

Some babies are pickier than others, so let them set the pace. Keep trying new options. They might hate raspberries one week, but love them the next.

Table Time Triumphs: Fun Ways to Foster Self-Feeding

Your independence-seeking tot will enjoy eating more when they can feed themselves. The first step is letting them explore their food. Textures won't seem so daunting when they've been able to squish, squash, and squeeze everything before they put it into their mouth.

Keep a silicone spoon and fork nearby so that they can get familiar with them. You'll need to help your baby dip and scoop initially, but they will catch on quickly. A fork is more challenging, because it takes some skill and precision to pierce food.

Toddlers crave autonomy, and your baby will love sitting at the table with you, watching and imitating how you eat.

Weaning

As your baby eats more solid food, they may start to self-wean.

Weaning is the gradual process of transitioning your baby from a breast milk or formula diet to solid foods. It's like gently nudging them out of the nest and into the wide world of culinary adventures.

Breast milk or formula will be your baby's main food source until they are 12 months old, and most major health organizations recommend sticking to that timeline. Weaning should be gradual and gentle, making it a positive experience for both Mom and baby.

There's no "normal" when it comes to weaning. Sometimes, moms are ready; sometimes, babies start the process. Go with the flow and do what's best for your family.

Snooze Solutions: Making the Move from Multiple Naps to a Solid Sleep Routine

Having regular meals means you can plan naps more easily. Your baby is probably sleeping two to three hours during two naps by this stage. By 18 months, they'll be down to one longer nap during lunchtime.

Unfortunately, some babies start dropping naps at around 12 months. Jackson noticed that his son consistently resisted his afternoon nap, struggled to fall asleep, and fought bedtime like his life depended on it. He tried shortening the naps and pushing them back 15 minutes, but after a few weeks, his son only took one nap a day.

With all the exciting new milestones your baby is hitting, they might experience sleep regression at this stage, affecting nap time. They may skip one nap, or sleep less during each nap. Maintain two naps for as long as possible, because learning to walk is exhausting. If you have to drop a nap, skip the morning and aim for a longer lunchtime nap.

From a Woman's Perspective: Actionable, Practical Steps to Take

This transitional time can be an emotional rollercoaster for moms. You're grappling with the fact that your baby is growing up, but you're also trying to figure out how to navigate the next phase of parenthood. Here are a few things that dads can do to make the transition easier.

Embrace the growing independence: Moms often find themselves grappling with conflicting emotions as their babies become more independent. While it's natural to feel a sense of pride in watching your little one explore the world, it can also be accompanied by a tinge of sadness as you realize they're growing up.

- **Action steps:** Show empathy and understanding towards your partner's feelings. Take the time to acknowledge and validate her emotions.

Be present: Moms value dads who are present and engaged in their children's lives, both physically and emotionally. It's about being there in body, mind, and spirit, actively participating in the precious moments and everyday routines of parenthood.

- **Action steps:** Make a conscious effort to be present and engaged with your baby and partner. Set aside dedicated quality time each day to bond with your little one, whether through playtime, bedtime routines, or simply cuddling on the couch. By being fully present, you'll create lasting memories and deepen your connection as a family.

Celebrate milestones together: From first steps to first words, every milestone is a cause for celebration in the journey of parenthood. Moms appreciate dads who are equally invested in commemorating these special moments and creating cherished memories as a family.

- **Action steps:** Whether it's capturing memories through photos and videos, planning a small family celebration, or simply sharing the joy and excitement of each milestone, your presence and enthusiasm will be deeply appreciated by your partner.

Key Takeaways

- Watching your baby cruise around the house is an exciting milestone, but it also means a potential sleep regression that can seriously mess up nap time.
- Your baby may already be transitioning to one nap a day.
- Top up your responsive parenting tank, because you're going to need it.
- Nurture your baby's autonomy, even when it feels hard and scary.
- Be bold and bountiful when it comes to finger food options.

Chapter Six

LITTLE PERSON, BIG FEELINGS: CULTIVATING EMOTIONAL INTELLIGENCE IN YOUR BABY'S FIRST YEAR

"My father didn't tell me how to live. He lived, and let me watch him do it."

— *Clarence Budington Kelland*

Buckle up and get ready to dive into the wonderfully wacky world of your baby's emotions. From the heart-melting smiles that make your day to the ear-splitting cries that test your sanity, it's a wild ride filled with surprises at every turn.

Parenting is all about emotional regulation—your baby's and your own. However, to teach your child what they need to know about feelings, you have to understand their cues and how to respond to them.

Emotional Expedition: Discovering the Milestones of Baby's First Year

From the time they are born, your baby experiences a wide variety of emotions, ranging from distress to interest and happiness. They won't understand your feelings yet, but they will know how you respond. Your baby will use their body language and facial expressions to tell you how they feel.

You'll start seeing real smiles at two to three months, and hearing those adorable baby giggles at four months. At five to six months, your baby will bury their face in your neck and pull away from strangers. Nine months mark the start of separation anxiety, tantrums, and big emotional reactions. At 12 months, your baby starts linking facial expressions with emotions.

During the first six months, your baby will be responding in the moment to immediate (usually physical) things. But by 12 months, they will be way more expressive and can probably use a few words.

Tips for Responding to Your Baby's Emotions

The best way to help your baby learn about emotional regulation is to control your emotions and respond with warmth and empathy. It's also important to notice their cues and give them what they need.

Are they rooting around on your chest? Feed them. Clenching their fists and frantically kicking their legs? Reduce stimulation. Throwing blocks and screaming? Validate their anger, but be firm with your boundaries.

It's a myth that you can spoil your baby by responding to their needs, so here are some hacks to help you jump on the emotional regulation train.

#87 - **Respond quickly.** Meeting your baby's needs quickly helps them make sense of the world. You give them a sense of safety and trust.

#88 - **Consider the "why."** It's easy to get frustrated with your baby, especially when they're having a very public meltdown. But what are they trying to communicate to you? Is there a reason they are crying? Our babies were "impossible" when tired, hungry, or overstimulated. We just needed to reframe their "bad" behavior and see it as communication.

#89 - **Take a breath.** Justin found himself shouting at his baby and getting impatient. It made him feel guilty, and only made his soon-to-be toddler more defiant. Our kids learn about emotions by mimicking our responses.

#90 - **Be consistent.** Your baby can't soothe themselves yet, but when you consistently respond to them, you help them learn how to regulate on their own.

Temperament Tales: Cracking the Code to Your Baby's Emotional World

Discovering your baby's temperament is like peeling back the layers of an onion—each new discovery reveals a new dimension of their unique personality. But just like an onion, some babies are sweet, others are spicy, and almost all of them will make you cry at some point. That being said, they also add flavor to your life, and their differences are what make them special.

Your baby's temperament is how they respond to the world. They may be easy, slow-to-warm, or difficult.

Connor's daughter was happy and busy, and he could take her anywhere without worrying about her freaking out. She was a baby with an easy temperament. His son was a chilled baby who would watch the world around him, but was slow to get involved. He was a slow-to-warm baby. Instead of forcing his son out of his comfort zone, Connor met him where he was. He created a safe and nurturing environment at home where he could explore at his own pace, free from pressure or expectations. He also respected his son's boundaries, gently encouraging him to interact with new people and experiences while always allowing him to retreat to the safety of his arms when needed.

Connor's brother Jensen, however, had a super reactive baby who hardly slept and refused most food. His baby had a difficult temperament. From the moment Liam entered the world, he made his presence known with a set of lungs that could rival a foghorn. No amount of rocking, singing, or shushing seemed to soothe him, leaving Jensen feeling like he was navigating uncharted waters without a compass.

Instead of succumbing to frustration, Jensen leaned into his role as Liam's dad with unwavering determination and a healthy dose of humor. He became a master of baby-wearing, strapping Liam to his chest and dancing around the living room like a seasoned pro. He also embraced the power of the "dad shush," honing his skills until he could soothe Liam to sleep with just a few gentle whispers. Perhaps most importantly, Jensen learned to trust his instincts and listen to his baby's cues. He discovered that Liam had a knack for picking up on his dad's mood. When Jensen remained calm and composed, Liam seemed to follow suit.

Setting the Tone: Modeling Emotional Regulation for Your Little One

Caught in the whirlwind of a tantrum from his 12-month-old daughter Lily, Stephen felt his frustration bubbling up. But instead of meeting her outburst with his own, he took a deep breath and tried to soothe Lily's storm with a calm voice and gentle reassurance. Slowly, her cries began to soften. At that moment, he knew he was teaching Lily an invaluable lesson: to navigate her emotions with patience and understanding.

Here are a few other ways to help your baby with emotional regulation:

Be mindful of your own emotions: Recognize and acknowledge your own feelings, both positive and negative. Your feelings are valid, and you need to feel them so that they don't explode all over your baby.

Demonstrate empathy and understanding: Empathy is a parenting superpower. Put yourself in your baby's shoes. It's tough being a little person in a world you don't always understand.

Communicate openly and honestly: Be open and honest with your baby about your own emotions and experiences. Use simple language and gestures to express your feelings, such as saying "I'm happy" while smiling or "I'm feeling frustrated" while taking deep breaths to calm down.

Practice active listening: Take the time to truly listen to your baby and pay attention to their cues and signals. Practice active listening by maintaining eye contact, nodding your head, and responding empathetically.

Show affection and comfort: Get your cuddle on to comfort and connect with your baby.

Be consistent and predictable. Create a safe and stable environment for your baby by responding consistently. Establish routines and rituals that provide security and predictability, and be there for your baby when they need you.

Toys That Teach: Nurturing Emotional Growth Through Play

Your baby uses all five of their senses to learn, explore, and develop. That means toys should be a sensory experience. Don't forget to make sure they're safe, because you know that EVERYTHING will end up in their mouth.

Soft and cuddly toys: That stuffed penguin your baby is obsessed with is vital to their emotional growth. It gives them a sense of comfort and can help them regulate when they feel upset or scared.

Interactive toys: Baby mirrors, peek-a-boo toys, and toys with buttons and switches are ideal for learning turn-taking, imitation, and communication.

Sensory toys: Choose toys that stimulate your baby's senses, such as rattles, textured balls, or different colors and patterns.

Role-play toys: Puppets, dolls, and pretend play help your baby develop empathy. Take Doctor Doctor, for example. Your toddler practices social skills and empathy as they try to "fix" you.

Books and storytelling: Reading and storytelling can help your baby develop language skills, cognitive abilities, and emotional understanding. They learn through the adventures and friendships of relatable characters, as well as their connection with you.

Outdoor play: Get outside! I can't emphasize this enough. Dadhood is made so much easier when you're outdoors. Outdoor play can help your baby develop a sense of curiosity, wonder, and connection. It also helps them test their emotional regulation skills out in the wild.

Emotional Roadmaps: Helping Your Child Understand Their Feelings

Emotional regulation might be one of the most essential skills you can teach your child. Have you seen an adult tantrum? It's not pretty. When your child is little, guiding them through emotions is tricky. But I promise the hard work pays off as they get older. We are definitely reaping the rewards now, so I will share some of our tried and tested methods for raising emotionally stable humans.

Validate their emotions: You need to let your child know there are no bad feelings, only bad reactions. It's okay for them to be upset that they can't have an extra cookie, but it's not okay to hit Mom or Dad for saying no.

Encourage open communication: This is tricky when they are young, but in general it means responding rather than reacting. If your child thinks they're going to get into trouble, you can bet they'll be hiding in the closet, munching on the cookie they stole.

Teach emotional vocabulary: Talk about feelings. If you're angry or happy, tell them. Explain what you're feeling so that they can start to make connections between facial expressions and emotions.

Model healthy emotional expression: Being aware of your emotional reactions is half the battle. Do you close cabinet doors with force or roll your eyes when you're mad? Your baby is watching everything you do, so start checking your behavior.

Teach coping skills: Teach your child healthy coping skills to help them manage their emotions and navigate difficult situations. Even small kids can learn breathing techniques and the power of positive affirmations.

Set limits and boundaries: Boundaries are another parenting must-have. They help you keep your cool and give your baby the guidelines they need to explore safely.

Grit Growth: Encouraging Tenacity and Perseverance in Your Baby

Did you know that grit is one of the biggest predictors of success in life? Grit is your ability to work toward a long-term goal, learn from mistakes, and persevere, even when things get tough.

Your baby won't understand grit the way adults do, but that doesn't mean you can't start helping them get more gritty.

Encourage exploration: Let them explore. By now, you know that your baby won't break, so let them be brave and do hard things. This helps build confidence and resilience by encouraging curiosity and a willingness to try new things.

Foster problem-solving skills: Don't make things too easy for them. Your baby is very capable of solving problems (like getting into the cookie jar unaided). Give them support and guidance, but allow them to experiment and figure things out on their own. This helps build resilience by teaching them to persist when facing challenges and setbacks.

Promote independence: Empower them with independent skills, such as feeding themselves, dressing themselves (as they grow older), and putting away toys.

Celebrate effort and progress: Praise your baby for trying, not just achieving. So much of what they learn comes from trying things, even when they don't get it right.

From a Woman's Perspective: Actionable, Practical Steps to Take

As a mom navigating the intricate world of emotions with our little one, there are some things I wish my partner had known when it came to teaching babies about feelings.

Emotions are valid: Babies experience a wide range of emotions, just like adults. From joy and excitement to frustration and sadness, each feeling is valid and deserves acknowledgment.

- **Action step:** When your baby is upset, acknowledge their feelings by saying something like, "I see you're feeling sad because your toy fell down. It's okay to feel that way."

Emotional development isn't a race: Comparing your baby to others isn't a good idea. Each baby develops at its own pace, and its temperament has a lot to do with it.

- **Action step:** Celebrate your baby for who they are and their personal milestones. Don't worry about what your friends' babies are doing.

Acknowledge and respect boundaries: Having a baby isn't always convenient, and they usually don't act in socially appropriate ways. But respecting your baby's boundaries teaches them the importance of consent and personal space.

- **Action step:** Respect your baby's cues for space and comfort. If they signal that they need space or don't want to be held, honor their boundaries to build trust and respect.

Key Takeaways

- Your baby will use their body language and facial expressions to let you know how they're feeling.
- During the first six months, your baby will be responding in the moment to immediate (usually physical) things. But by 12 months, they will be way more expressive and use a few words.
- The best way to help your baby learn about emotional regulation is to control your own emotions and respond with warmth and empathy to them.
- Your baby's temperament is how they respond to the world. They may be easy, slow-to-warm, or difficult.
- Emotional regulation and grit are two of the most important skills you can teach your child.

Part Two
BE THE BEST DAD YOU CAN BE

Chapter Seven
FROM TWO TO THREE: A DAD'S GUIDE TO HARMONIZING FAMILY AND RELATIONSHIP

"A good father is one of the most unsung, unpraised, unnoticed, and yet one of the most valuable assets in our society."

— *Billy Graham*

Brace yourself for the whirlwind of emotions that come with a new addition to the family. It's common to feel overwhelmed, excited, and even a bit anxious as you adjust to your new role as a dad. Like Justin, Alec, Stephen, and all the other dads mentioned throughout the book, you'll find yourself having to adapt and grow into your new role and responsibilities. It can be challenging, but it's a path that thousands of dads have walked before you.

Parenthood is all about growth and change. How cool is that? You constantly get to push your boundaries and challenge yourself to be a better version of you. It's a journey that will help you deepen your relationship with your partner as you embark on the adventure of raising your little human. Be patient with yourself and your partner as you navigate this transition together.

The most essential parts of juggling life and dadhood are having fun, embracing the learning curve, and laughing at every opportunity.

New Roles, New Challenges: Navigating Family Dynamics Post-Baby

You probably noticed that your baby was already changing things before they even popped into the world. There's no denying that adding another member to your family is a mammoth adjustment. You essentially become a parent overnight. Yes, you have nine months to prep and plan, but parenthood arrives like a freight train, and you need to get on board quickly.

While I was standing with my friends around a barbecue, we talked about the unexpected relationship changes that came with having a baby. For most of us, the jump from a partnership of two to a family of three was hectic. Many of us felt a bit sidelined as our baby took center stage, not to mention the exhaustion, constant time crunch, endless loads of laundry, and lack of sex.

Our relationships went from being connected and intimate to transactional.

"Did you buy extra wipes?"
"Have you washed the bottles?"
"Can you do the 11:00 p.m. feed?"
"Please pass the breast pads."

And then Jason dropped an interesting bomb that gave us all food for thought. "Have you heard of patrescence?" None of us had. Patrescence is the process of becoming a father. It's the push and pull you feel between wanting to be a fantastic dad and the person you were before dadhood. Moms also go through matrescence as they navigate motherhood. That means you and your partner are going through a monumental metamorphosis, all while being sleep-deprived and stressed about money, parenting styles, and getting your baby into that prestigious preschool down the block.

UCLA health psychiatrist Misty Richards, MD, MS, says new parents should use the three Rs to navigate changing relationship dynamics.

- **Regulate:** Check in with your emotions so you respond, not react.

- **Relate:** Opt for empathy as you work together to conquer parenting.
- **Reason:** Calmly chat about issues and how to resolve them.

Remember, you are getting to know both your baby and who you are in your new role. That's a lot, so be patient and give yourself grace.

Work and Play: Achieving Balance in the Busy Parenting Journey

Finding the right balance between your career and family life can feel like a juggling act. Still, with some planning and flexibility, you can make it work!

Flexible work arrangements: We live in an exciting time of diverse work options, such as remote work, flexible hours, and parental leave. Chat with HR or your boss about your options. The goal is to be present for your family while meeting your professional obligations.

Prioritize what is important to you: That goes for both work and home. As much as you think you can do it all…you can't. With limited time and energy, it's essential to prioritize your commitments and focus on what matters most. Identify your top priorities at work and home. Don't hesitate to delegate tasks or say no to non-essential time drains.

Create a family calendar: Keep track of important dates, appointments, and events with a shared family calendar. This is hack #91, and you will use it every day for the next 18 years.

Whether it's doctor's appointments, playdates, or family outings, having a centralized calendar ensures everyone is on the same page and helps you stay organized amidst the chaos of family life. It's like the command center of your home that keeps things running smoothly.

Set boundaries: You can't juggle work and fatherhood without boundaries. Stephen suggested I put my phone on airplane mode when I got home. He said the most important people in my life were at home with me, and that work emails and social media were stealing precious moments from my time with them.

Switch to dad mode: Moving from the boardroom to the baby room can be hard, so why not have a routine that tells your brain to activate dad mode? It could be a podcast on the drive home, a quick gym session, or a special greeting for your partner and baby.

Love in the Time of Diapers: Prioritizing Your Partnership

The first year of parenthood can strain even the strongest relationships. You've got to dig deep and commit 100% to learning and growing together. It's a lot, but with patience, communication, and a sprinkle of humor, you can weather the storm together.

Communication is key: Open and honest communication is the foundation of a healthy relationship. Make time to check in with each other regularly, share your thoughts and feelings, and deal with any issues. When you're not communicating effectively, wires get crossed and chaos ensues. Take it from someone who's been there—you don't want to do that to yourself. Just say the things and have the hard chats.

Quality time, not quantity: It may feel like you're constantly short on time...and actually, you are. I'm not going to sugarcoat it. But guess what? Parenting brings out your creative side and lets you find fun ways to connect. Whether it's cooking dinner together, going for a walk, or simply cuddling on the couch, find moments to connect and strengthen your bond.

Keep the romance alive: Don't let parenthood extinguish the flames of romance. Make an effort to keep the romance alive by planning date nights (think living room picnic rather than a night on the town) and surprising each other with thoughtful gestures. Flora and I would leave love notes for each other. It was something we did when we first started dating, and it was a special way to add some spice to our daily "transactions."

Divide and conquer: Share the responsibilities of parenthood and divide tasks based on each other's strengths and preferences. Whether it's changing diapers, doing laundry, or soothing a fussy baby, teamwork makes the dream work.

Pennies and Pacifiers: Navigating Parenthood on a Budget

Parenthood doesn't have to break the bank. It will try to do so, but with some creativity and resourcefulness, you can raise your child without blowing your budget.

Create a baby budget: Sit down with your partner and create a realistic budget for baby-related expenses, including diapers, formula, clothing, and childcare. Are there areas where you can cut costs or find ways to save money?

Prioritize the important things: What your family considers important may look different to other families. For example, Flora likes to buy local produce at the farmers market, and I like expensive coffee beans. These are non-negotiables for us. That means we compromise in other areas, like going on fancy holidays.

Embrace hand-me-downs: Babies grow like weeds and quickly outgrow their clothes, toys, and gear. Save money by accepting hand-me-downs from friends or family, or shopping for gently used items at thrift stores or online marketplaces.

Choose multi-use baby items: There are so many things that you use only once before your baby outgrows them, so choose items with multiple uses, or products that will transition with your baby. Opt for a backpack-style diaper bag that leaves your hands free and transitions well with a busy toddler. A convertible car seat is also a winning option. This is a car seat that can transition from rear-facing to forward-facing, and eventually to a booster seat, accommodating your child's growth and ensuring safety throughout the different stages of life.

Meal planning and batch cooking: Save time and money by planning and cooking nutritious meals for your family in batches. Stock your freezer with homemade baby food, soups, and casseroles that can be easily reheated on busy days, and avoid the temptation of expensive takeout or convenience foods.

Find free family activities: Look for free or low-cost activities and events in your community that you can enjoy as a family. Whether visiting a local park, attending storytime at the library, or hosting a playdate with other parents, there are plenty of budget-friendly ways to have fun and bond with your baby.

From a Woman's Perspective: Actionable, Practical Steps to Take

The journey of matrescence is transformational but challenging. Here are some things I wish my partner had known as we rediscovered each other in our new parenting roles.

Be present and engaged: Your active presence and engagement in your family's life are vital to your child's development and your partner's well-being. Put down your phone, turn off the TV, and be fully present in the moments that matter most.

- **Action step:** Dedicate uninterrupted time each day to your family. Whether it's reading a bedtime story, playing together on the floor, or going for a family walk, these moments of connection are precious and fleeting.

Self-care is non-negotiable: As you prioritize your family's needs, don't forget to prioritize your own well-being, as well. Self-care isn't selfish. In fact, skipping self-care makes it difficult for your partner to set aside the guilt and look after herself.

- **Action step:** Make self-care a priority in your daily routine. Whether it's going for a run, practicing meditation, or simply taking a moment to breathe, prioritize activities that nourish your mind, body, and soul.

#92 - Use self-care time as part of your dad mode transition.

Support means everything: Your support as a dad is invaluable to your partner and your family. Whether it's lending a hand with household chores, offering a listening ear after a tough day, or simply being there to share the load, your support makes all the difference.

- **Action step:** Take the initiative to tackle household tasks without being asked. Whether changing diapers, preparing meals, or tidying up around the house, your proactive support will lighten your partner's load and show her how much you care.

Key Takeaways

- Your baby will change the dynamic of your relationship, but it's not all bad! As your baby adapts to life outside the womb, so will you and your partner find your new normal.
- Patrescence is a real thing, so go easy on yourself as you adjust to your new role.
- Remember the three Rs: regulate, relate, reason.
- Have a ritual that helps you switch to dad mode.
- Keep the romance alive with quality time. Get creative and make time for each other.
- You shouldn't go into debt for your baby. Use our budget hacks to help you save money and a lot of stress.

Chapter Eight
BABY ON BOARD: A DAD'S GUIDE TO GETTING OUT OF THE HOUSE WITH A BABY

"A dad is someone who wants to catch you before you fall, but instead picks you up, brushes you off, and lets you try again."

— *Unknown*

You're all set to head out with your little one, armed with diapers, snacks, and a sense of adventure. But just as you're about to hit the road, your baby decides it's the perfect time for a diaper blowout!

This was a pretty common occurrence in our house. Getting out the door with your pint-sized sidekick can feel like preparing for a mission to Mars. From wrangling squirmy arms into jackets to strategically packing the diaper bag with more precision than a game of Tetris, every outing comes with its own set of challenges and triumphs. And as they get older, you'll have to deal with a toddler who wants to put on their own shoes (you laugh now, but it's a thing) and loudly give their opinion about your choice of outing.

But with patience, perseverance, pro tips, and snacks, you can figure out how to make it out of the house and have a successful adventure with your child.

Dad's Ultimate Outing Playbook: Making Memories on the Go

Getting out as a family is exciting, and a great way to make special memories. But as Jensen and Connor discovered, taking your little buddy adventuring can be a challenge. They decided to get the cousins together at the park, but they underestimated how much planning was required to make memories instead of making a mess.

Here are some pro tips to help you find family outing success instead of ending up with crying kids and irate dads like Jensen and Connor.

Go with the flow: Babies are unpredictable creatures, so be prepared to roll with whatever curveballs they throw your way. Sometimes, you have to give up the idea of what you thought your outing would look like and embrace the imperfect moment you find yourself in. There's magic in those moments.

Make safety a priority: Whether you're on the beach or at the playground, always prioritize your baby's safety. Keep a close eye on them at all times, and be prepared to swoop in at a moment's notice.

Consider the environment: Pack the right gear for where you're going. I'm not just talking about extra clothes, diapers, and a sun hat, because those should be diaper bag staples. If you're going to be out all day, then you may want a stroller for nap time. If you're going somewhere busy and less accessible, then opt for a baby carrier or sling. There's nothing worse than carting a stroller around somewhere with a million stairs.

Pack snacks: Don't let your baby or your partner get hangry (if you know, you know). Hunger can turn even the calmest baby into a tyrant, so have a snack available.

Avoid outing overload: Getting out of the house is exciting, but don't go too crazy. Small kids get overwhelmed and overstimulated quickly (word of warning, so do their parents), so space out your outings. Kids enjoy routine and familiarity, so go to similar outing spots. This will help your baby not feel overwhelmed, and you'll know what to expect.

Keep to your routine: If you can work outings around feed and nap times, then you have a higher chance of outing success. Leaving the house is a lot of excitement, so maintaining your baby's usual touchpoints can keep them regulated and ready for adventure.

Celebrate the small victories: From successfully navigating a busy museum to mastering the art of the family selfie, celebrate every small victory along the way. Parenthood is all about embracing the little moments that make life special.

Conquering Public Spaces: Dad Edition

People? Germs? Why would I want to be out in public with my baby?

Those were my first thoughts when I had to navigate a public place with my baby. Natalie was chunky and cute, and I knew she would get loads of attention, but I wasn't ready to have strangers get up close and personal with her.

So what is a dad to do? Well, for starters, keep your trips short. Think of it as a test run as you learn what works and what doesn't, and build up confidence. You need realistic expectations of what you and your baby can handle, and short trips help you keep things real.

Once I had been out and about a couple of times as a new dad, I realized that a lot of my anxiety was about other people's reactions to my baby being, well, a baby. Don't be afraid to stake your claim in public spaces. Whether you're changing a diaper in a crowded restroom or feeding in a busy cafe, remember that you have every right to be there.

Also, people are curious creatures. Don't let the inevitable stares or comments get to you. Just smile, nod, and carry on like the confident dad you are. Try to find family-friendly spots. Look for cafes, parks, and other public spaces where you won't feel like you're under a microscope. These places are a godsend when you need a break or a change of scenery.

As your baby gets older, you can use public places as a learning experience. Behavior, emotional regulation, and independence are best learned through doing. But sometimes, you just need a quiet moment without having to have eyes in the back of your head. That's why a bag of distractions is a must. Board books, blocks, toys, and even a device are essential backups for touchy toddlers.

One last thing: When being out in public seems too much, take a deep breath, roll with the punches, and remember that this, too, shall pass.

Baby's First Adventure: Navigating the World with Your Little Explorer

Whether you're hitting the road or taking to the skies, traveling with a baby requires some serious strategy.

Taking to the Skies

If you're brave enough to fly with your baby, waiting a few months is best. Realistically, neither you nor your partner will be interested in leaving the comfort of your sofa in those early weeks, anyway. But if you do have travel on the brain, flying after two months means less risk of serious bacterial infection, and your baby would have had a few more vaccinations.

Flying can seem daunting. You'll know why if you've ever been stuck on a plane with a screaming baby. But don't panic. Most people have been there and will be sympathetic—not to mention that most people fly with headphones.

There are a few logistical things to consider when you fly with a baby, like what to do with your stroller, carry-on requirements, and having the right car seat. Phone the airline ahead of time so you aren't caught unprepared. Also, check that your car seat has an FAA-approved label, making it safe for flying.

Hitting the Road

If flying freaks you out, there's always a road trip. Traveling by car gives you more control, as Tom discovered firsthand.

Tom and Sarah were embarking on their first road trip with their baby, Max. As they hit the highway, Max's cries echoed through the car. Tom glanced at Sarah with a nervous smile, silently wondering if they had bitten off more than they could chew.

But they weren't completely unprepared. Instead of panicking, Sarah turned on some nursery rhymes. With Max happily engrossed in the songs, Tom and Sarah breathed a sigh of relief and settled into the rhythm of the road.

They packed a travel tray filled with Max's favorite toys and snacks, turning the backseat into a mini-entertainment center. Every couple of hours, they pulled over for a break, stretching their legs and allowing Max to burn off some energy. And if they were being honest, those breaks were just as much for Mom and Dad as they were for the baby.

What can we learn from Tom and Sarah? Do your prep before your trip. Keep stops in mind as you plan your route, and work the stops around naps. Keep everyone hydrated, fed, and distracted with loads of entertainment. Finally, be prepared to sing Twinkle Twinkle more times than you can count.

Tips for Dads on the Move: Mastering Parenthood on the Fly

Ever tried juggling a baby, a diaper bag, and your keys all at once? It's like a circus act, except it's not funny.

Here are some pro tips to keep you cool, calm, and collected on your outings.

Master the art of packing: It's all about the essentials. Pack diapers, wipes, snacks, and a change of clothes like you're prepping for a mission to Mars. Bonus points for a portable changing pad and some hand sanitizer for those impromptu diaper changes.

Embrace the backpack: Ditch the over-the-shoulder diaper bag for a sleek backpack. Trust me, it's a game-changer. You'll have both hands free for baby wrangling, and you'll look effortlessly cool while doing it.

Strategic snacks: Hangry baby = no bueno. Keep a stash of baby-friendly snacks on hand to ward off any hunger-induced meltdowns. #93 Pack a few extras for yourself. You'll thank me later.

Layer up: Layering is key when it comes to outfitting your little explorer for the great outdoors. You never know when the weather might decide to throw you a curveball, so be prepared with plenty of options to keep your baby snug as a bug or cool as a cucumber.

Keep the car stocked: Keep your car stocked with all the essentials—diapers, wipes, blankets, and a stash of baby-friendly snacks to ward off any hunger-induced meltdowns. #94 Don't forget to top up the gas tank, while you're at it. You never know when you might need to make a quick escape!

Know your baby's limits: Every little adventurer has their limits, and it's important to know when it's time to call it a day. Keep an eye out for signs of fatigue or discomfort. Don't be afraid to pivot your plans if your baby needs a little R&R. Remember, it's better to cut your adventure short than to push your baby (and you) beyond their limits.

From a Woman's Perspective: Actionable, Practical Steps to Take

Often, the burden of getting out of the house with everyone looking cute can fall on moms. If you've ever seen your partner putting mascara on in the car, just know she was rushed out of the house and could have used your help. Here are a few things I wish my partner had known. Hopefully, these tips can help you bring your A game to family outings.

Teamwork makes the dream work: While it may seem like she's got everything under control, your partner would appreciate your help. From carrying the diaper bag to soothing your little one during those inevitable meltdowns, your support means the world to her.

- **Action step:** Offer to take on specific tasks during outings, such as packing the diaper bag or handling navigation duties.

Making memories trumps perfection: While you may strive for picture-perfect outings, it's the memories you make along the way that truly matter. Family outings should be more about family than the outing.

- **Action step:** Focus on creating meaningful memories during outings rather than doing everything "right." Embrace the messiness and spontaneity of spending time together.

Embrace the unpredictability: Parenthood is full of surprises, and outings are no exception. Instead of letting unexpected twists and turns derail your plans, embrace unpredictability and see where the adventure takes you. Who knows—you might just stumble upon your next favorite family hangout spot!

- **Action step:** Approach each outing with a sense of adventure and curiosity. By staying flexible and open-minded, you can help your partner embrace any changes in the plans.

Key Takeaways

- Embrace baby-wearing for hands-free convenience.
- While planning is essential, don't be afraid to embrace spur-of-the-moment adventures and make the most of unexpected opportunities.
- Understanding your baby's schedule and limits helps you plan outings at optimal times to minimize fussiness.
- Navigate public spaces with confidence and patience.
- Prioritize safety and capture precious memories on family outings.
- Your active involvement as a dad is invaluable and deeply appreciated.
- Keeping a well-stocked diaper bag and having a checklist of essentials ensures you're prepared for any adventure with your baby.
- Don't forget to snap photos and videos to document your outings and create lasting memories with your little one.

Chapter Nine
TROUBLESHOOTING GUIDE FOR DAD CHALLENGES

"Having children is like living in a frat house—nobody sleeps, everything's broken, and there's a lot of throwing up."

— *Ray Romano*

If you're reading this chapter first because you need fast answers, I get it. The adventure of being a new dad certainly has some unexpected detours. But those detours can be filled with unique insights and cherished moments.

You know how they say it's the journey, not the destination? Well, that's particularly true when it comes to parenthood. Every day is a chance to experience new things with your baby as you learn and grow together. Having a baby doesn't make you a parent, but raising one does.

But that doesn't mean you don't need some help and solid advice for those tricky moments—and that's what this chapter is all about. From dealing with in-laws to busting some popular dad myths, this chapter is full of juicy nuggets to answer your most pressing questions.

Navigating the Highs and Hiccups of Extended Family Dynamics

Navigating the wild and wonderful world of in-laws and extended family is a journey that can be both exhilarating and exhausting.

Balancing relationships with extended family members is a delicate dance, like walking a tightrope while juggling flaming torches. On one hand, we want to foster strong connections and create lasting memories with our loved ones. On the other hand, we also need to set boundaries to ensure our own sanity.

How do we strike the perfect balance between bonding with our in-laws and keeping the peace?

It all comes down to communication, setting boundaries with love and intention, and developing thicker skin. You'll never make everyone happy, and it's not your job to do so. Your priority is your little family, first and foremost.

Communication

When it comes to dealing with in-laws and extended family, communication is your best friend. Whether it's discussing plans for holiday gatherings or addressing concerns about boundaries, open and honest communication is essential.

#95 - When there is something sensitive to discuss, **talk to your own parents**. You can't offend your partner's parents if you aren't the one talking to them. Setting boundaries can be hard enough without throwing in all the baggage that comes with complex relationships.

You should think about having regular check-ins with your partner to discuss any concerns or issues that arise with extended family members. Remember when I said that you should have hard conversations? Well, this is one of those times. By staying on the same page and presenting a united front, you can tackle any challenges together. Things will only get stickier if you're each siding with your own family.

#96 - Kill them with kindness, even when they're driving you nuts. It's easy to make a snarky comment when your father-in-law is giving you "advice" on properly barbecuing ribs or maintaining the siding, but remember, your child is watching your interactions.

You might not love your father-in-law, but your baby does. Choose kindness whenever you can.

Set Boundaries (and Stick to Them)

Don't be afraid to set clear boundaries with your extended family members. Stephen was always my go-to friend when it came to boundaries. Remember his airplane mode suggestion? Parenting gold. So, when I needed help enforcing a boundary with Flora's mom, he was the person I turned to.

His advice? Come up with a list of non-negotiables. What are the things that you aren't willing to compromise on? I had a chat with Flora (another hard conversation), and we came up with ground rules we weren't willing to budge on. Some of them were controversial, like spending Christmas Eve alone. Others were easier to understand, like calling before visiting.

We put our core boundaries in an email and sent it to our nearest and dearest. That way, they had time to process it, and it prevented any arguments. Consistently enforcing boundaries has been a game-changer for our family dynamics.

Pick Your Battles

Not every disagreement with your in-laws is worth going to war over. Sometimes, it's better to let minor issues slide and focus on maintaining healthy relationships.

Before engaging in a battle royale with your in-laws, ask yourself: Is this issue worth the potential fallout? If not, consider letting it go and focusing your energy on more important matters.

Find Common Ground

Despite our differences, we usually have some common ground with our extended family members. Whether it's a shared love of gardening, a passion for cooking, or a mutual disdain for kale, finding common interests can help bridge the gap and strengthen relationships. If you really can't find anything, remember that you both love your baby and want the best for them.

#97 - Include them in small ways. Your extended family and in-laws just want to be involved and feel needed. My mom gave me great advice once. She said, "When Flora phoned and asked for advice about a recipe, I felt needed and valued. The small things can make the biggest impact."

When in Doubt, Laugh

Last but certainly not least, don't forget to keep a healthy dose of humor handy when navigating the murky waters of family dynamics. Sometimes, all you can do is laugh—at the absurdity of it all, the chaos of family gatherings, and the quirks that make each of us unique.

When things start to get tense or overwhelming, take a step back and find the humor in the situation. Crack a joke, share a funny story, or simply laugh at the absurdity of it all. After all, laughter is the best medicine—especially when dealing with in-laws and extended family.

Mythbusting Fatherhood: Dispelling Common Misconceptions About Dads

Dad myths are the worst because they freak you out about fatherhood before it even begins. As it turns out, having a baby isn't a fate worse than death. Yes, it'll turn your world upside down, but it will also launch you into the best adventure of your life.

I was terrified before our first baby arrived, and these were some of the common myths that made it worse.

Myth: Fathers Are Secondary Parents

Let's address this misconception head-on. The idea that dads are somehow "secondary" parents is about as outdated as dial-up Internet. Yet, despite the strides we've made in redefining traditional gender roles, this myth still lingers like a stubborn stain on a onesie.

Parenthood isn't about who ranks higher. It's a tag-team effort, a partnership forged in sleepless nights and endless diaper changes. You and your partner each bring your unique strengths to the parenting table, creating a dynamic duo greater than the sum of its parts.

So, why does the myth of dads as secondary parents persist? Maybe it's because movies and TV bombard us with images of moms as the caring ones and dads as the providers. Or perhaps it's because society has a hard time letting go of outdated gender norms that pigeonhole men into the role of breadwinner rather than nurturer.

You're not playing second fiddle. Being a dad is about showing up, stepping up, and giving it your all, day in and day out. It's about changing diapers at 3:00 am, holding firm on boundaries, and rocking your baby to sleep when your partner has had enough.

Let's put this myth to bed once and for all. You're not a secondary parent. You are a dad, a superhero in disguise, with a cape covered in spit-up and other unmentionables. You're raising the next generation of changemakers with your partner, one diaper change at a time.

#98 - Plan a special "dad's day out" where you and your baby explore new places and activities together, just the two of you. Make it a monthly ritual.

Myth: Dads Aren't as Nurturing as Moms

Nurturing isn't reserved for just moms. As a unique dad, you can nurture your baby in a unique way. Maybe it's turning diaper changes into a game or giving impromptu piggyback rides around the living room. Either way, your special brand of nurturing is about caring for and protecting your baby, just like Mom.

Moms may have that special touch for soothing a crying baby or kissing boo boos, but dads bring their own brand of magic to the table. Every tickle fight, wrestling match, and bike ride gives your child something vital for growth and happiness.

It's sad that this myth is even a thing. Dads can be nurturing and strong. One could argue that showing softness and vulnerability is what makes dads strong. We've been conditioned to see dadhood through a narrow lens, which doesn't leave much room for dads to shine. But it's time to change that.

Dads are just as capable of nurturing their children as moms, so let's ditch the stereotypes and embrace the reality that fathers offer something incredible in how they nurture and love their babies.

#99 - Create a ritual with your baby that is just for the two of you. Maybe it's how you put them to bed or greet them in the morning.

Myth: Dads Are Incompetent When It Comes to Childcare

While this is a myth to some extent, there are still a lot of dads who don't know their asses from their elbows when it comes to certain parts of childcare. But the idea that dads are glorified babysitters isn't fair to most modern dads, who are hands-on and involved. Commercials and TV shows depicting clueless dads have perpetuated the idea that childcare is "women's work" and dads just aren't cut out for it. This is FALSE. You can have just as many parenting skills as your partner. Luckily, dads are stepping up with diaper changes, midnight feedings, playtime, and bedtime routines, and knocking it out of the park every single day.

Looking after your baby is something you can learn and practice. It's not an innate superpower, it's a choice.

#100 - Take on more roles that most people consider "mom territory." Make that pediatrician appointment, puree some vegetables to freeze for quick meals, or take your baby to a playgroup.

Myth: Fathers Don't Form Close Bonds With Babies

There's a misconception floating around that dads are somehow less equipped to form close bonds with their babies than moms. In reality, dads are more than capable of forging deep, meaningful connections with their little ones from day one.

Moms are usually seen as the primary caregivers, with dads being relegated to "fun parents." But the truth is that dads form bonds with their babies in a different way, and it's just as powerful and enduring as the bond between a mother and child.

Each time you cuddle your baby skin-to-skin, breathe in that baby smell, or help them regulate their big feelings, you're strengthening your bond with them. You may not have carried your baby inside your body, but when you respond to their needs with love and cuddles, your bond grows and deepens.

#101 - Wear your baby whenever possible. Being close, responding to their needs, and taking them along on daily adventures is a simple way to get your bond on.

Myth: Dads Will Parent Like Their Dads

If you didn't have the kind of dad you can look up to, that's okay. Sure, the way you were raised will affect you, but you can still rewrite the playbook.

You are constantly evolving, learning, and adapting to be the partner and father your family needs. You can take bits and pieces from your own upbringing, sprinkle in some new ideas and strategies, and forge your own parenting path.

Something that makes me super happy is seeing dads break free from the constraints of tradition and expectations and embrace a more individualized approach to parenting. While it's natural to be influenced by your upbringing, remember that every family is different, and there's no one "right" way to parent. Take the lessons you learned from your dad—good and not-so-good—and use them as a foundation to build your own parenting style. Be open to new ideas and approaches. Don't be afraid to break the mold.

#102 - Make a list of things you love about your dad, as well as things you don't want to bring into your parenting. It's hard to look honestly at your parents, but you can't change parenting patterns without identifying them first.

Myth: Dad's Don't Need Support

There's a pervasive myth that dads don't need support when it comes to parenting. They're like lone wolves, navigating the wilds of fatherhood all on their own. But the truth is, parenting is tough and no one can do it alone.

Dads need support just as much as moms do, because they face unique challenges that can leave them feeling overwhelmed and isolated. The idea that asking for help is a sign of weakness and that real men should be able to handle anything that comes their way with stoic resolve is seriously outdated.

There's strength in vulnerability, and asking for support is a sign of courage, not weakness. Dads deserve a safe space to share their struggles, seek advice, and connect with other fathers. Let's bust this myth wide open and create a space where dads feel supported, valued, and empowered to be the best parents they can be.

#103 - Sometimes, all it takes is a virtual or in-person meet-up with other dads going through similar experiences. If you haven't already, find your people.

Unraveling Common Concerns and Misconceptions

Something that comes up repeatedly in my dad group and with my friends is common concerns that new dads have. Most revolve around balancing all their responsibilities, putting their childhoods behind them, and bonding with their babies. Luckily, we've already covered those topics, so if you were worried about these things, you've got some solid advice in your dad's tool belt.

But other concerns aren't spoken about enough.

So many dads are worried about messing up. And guess what? You're going to…all the time! That's what being a parent and a person is about. You mess up, learn, and try again. We all have stories of losing our cool, disappointing our partners, and emptying a whole powder bottle on our newborn (or is that just me?). But the good news is that your baby and your partner don't need perfection; they just need progress. They need you to keep trying and showing up in all your imperfect dadness.

I've also had vulnerable conversations with dads about their relationships. Birth and motherhood dramatically shift things for your partner, and sex is probably the last thing on her mind. It can be a touchy subject and a sore point as you both navigate the first year of parenthood. There's no right or wrong way to handle this situation. My best advice is to find other ways to be intimate that don't involve sex if your partner isn't ready. Cuddling, holding hands, giving massages, or simply sitting close together can help you feel connected and loved without the pressure of sex.

Sometimes, it's not the fears and concerns that make new dads freak out. Often, the misconceptions about dadhood are what cause issues.

There's a pervasive misconception that dads need to have it all together all the time. The truth is that parenthood is messy, chaotic, and full of ups and downs. It's okay to ask for help and to embrace the imperfections of the journey. Social media perpetuates the idea that dads should do it all, and it's easy to fall into the trap of comparing yourself to other parents who seem to have it all figured out. But social media is little more than a curated snippet of someone's life, and you never really know what mess lies behind those little squares.

Another common misconception that has new dads in panic mode is that their social lives die when their babies are born. But that's not true. While it may seem like your days of wild nights and spontaneous adventures are over, your social life is merely taking on a new form—one that involves less beer pong and more baby monitors. Your new party scene involves playdates at the local park, where the snacks are organic and the conversation revolves around sleep schedules and diaper blowouts. But something cool about this new adventure is that your social circle transforms into a support group of fellow dads who understand the struggles and triumphs of parenthood. Who needs happy hour when you have a group chat full of dad jokes and parenting memes?

FAQs You Never Knew You Needed

FAQ: Is it normal for my baby to cry so much?

Yes, babies cry—a lot! It's their primary mode of communication, and it doesn't necessarily mean something is wrong. Trust your instincts and seek help if you're concerned about excessive crying.

FAQ: Is it normal to feel like I have no idea what I'm doing?

You bet! Parenthood doesn't come with an instruction manual (but wouldn't that be handy?). Embrace the learning curve and have faith that you'll figure it out as you go. Remember, even seasoned parents are making it up as they go along!

FAQ: What's the deal with baby poop?

Ah, the age-old mystery of baby bowel movements! From mustard yellow to army green, baby poop comes in a range of shades. As long as it's soft and your little one seems comfortable, you're golden (just like their poop).

FAQ: How many diapers does one baby actually need?

A lot! Stock up on diapers like you're preparing for the apocalypse, because those little bundles of joy have a knack for going through them at lightning speed.

FAQ: What's the protocol for handling unsolicited parenting advice?

We've all been there—nodding politely while silently screaming inside and trying not to let that eye roll happen on the outside. Smile, nod, and do what works best for you and your baby. Remember, you're the expert on your own little one.

FAQ: Is it normal to feel jealous when the baby gets more attention than me?

Absolutely! Babies monopolize everyone's time. Remember, you may have lost the spotlight, but you've gained a tiny admirer who thinks you're the coolest person on the planet.

FAQ: Can I blame the baby for my sudden urge to buy a minivan?

That's a given. Just tell everyone it's for "safety reasons," but secretly revel in the extra legroom and cup holders.

FAQ: Is it okay if I use my baby as an excuse to get out of social events?

Every parent I know has done this. Just perfect your "sorry, can't make it, baby duty calls" face for maximum effectiveness.

FAQ: Can I still enjoy my hobbies with a baby around?

This can be tricky, but it's not impossible. Just be prepared for some creative multitasking. Whether your baby watches you tinker in the garage or you buy a jogging stroller and take them for a run, there's always a way to incorporate your hobbies into dad life.

FAQ: Is it normal to feel overwhelmed by all the conflicting parenting advice out there?

It would be weird if you didn't. Remember, every baby is unique, and what works for one may not work for another. Trust your instincts, lean on your support network, and don't be afraid to laugh off the well-meaning but unsolicited advice.

From a Woman's Perspective: Actionable, Practical Steps to Take

Being a new dad is overwhelming and scary. Trust me, we women are experiencing the same mix of emotions. I wish my partner had been open about his fears and concerns—firstly, so we could comfort and support each other, and secondly, so that I understood what he was going through. Here's what I wish new dads understood.

Self-care for dad: Self-care isn't selfish—it's essential for your well-being and ability to show up for your family.

- **Action step:** Whether it's taking a walk, indulging in a hobby, or seeking professional support, prioritize your mental, emotional, and physical health.

Maintaining intimacy: We crave connection. You are our safe place and the person we turn to when it feels like we're drowning.

- **Action step:** Find creative ways to nurture your relationship amidst the demands of parenthood. Schedule date nights, share affectionate gestures, and spend quality time together.

Navigating family and friend dynamics: Your partner needs your help, especially when she feels pulled in a million different directions. She knows that friends and family mean well, but she can struggle with the conflicting demands of your baby, family, and you.

- **Action step:** Communicate openly with friends and family about your parenting preferences and boundaries. Have your partner's back when she feels overwhelmed with the demands everyone's making on her.

Key Takeaways

- Communication and kindness are what you need to navigate complex family dynamics and in-law relationships.
- Pick your battles with your friends, family, and partner. Part of being a dad is learning how to go with the flow and when to fight for your convictions.
- Dad myths suck, and most of them aren't true. They make you stress about fatherhood and take energy away from learning how to be the dad you want to be.
- You're going to make mistakes. There's no such thing as a perfect parent or partner. Perfection isn't the goal; connection is.
- Your relationship with your partner will change, and it may take time to get back to your pre-baby level of intimacy. But having a baby together connects you in a way nothing else can, and it's pretty darn special.

Conclusion
THE END OF THE BOOK BUT NOT YOUR JOURNEY

Fatherhood is filled with a magic that can't be explained, only felt. From the exhilarating highs to the challenging lows, the first year of fatherhood is a transformative experience unlike any other.

Whether you're navigating the sleepless nights of the newborn stage or embarking on the adventures of toddlerhood, I hope The New Dad Code has given you the tips and hacks you need to feel empowered and confident.

With each chapter we explored a new aspect of fatherhood. We looked at the challenges, but we also highlighted the joys and added a good dose of humor and a sprinkle of helpful hints. From those early weeks with a helpless newborn to dealing with a defiant and active almost-toddler, the overarching theme of each chapter is finding your feet by doing dadhood your own way. There's so much pressure on dads today, but your child doesn't need a picture-perfect father. They need one who shows up, learns from his mistakes, and loves them with his whole heart.

Being a dad will challenge you more than anything you've ever done. Not only does it force you to take a hard look at yourself, but it also changes your relationship with your partner. And to make it more complicated, fatherhood is for life. You never stop being a parent, but you do grow into it. I hope this book has helped make some of that growth a bit easier.

So, here's to you. Here's to the late-night feedings and the early-morning cuddles. Here's to the messy diaper changes and the endless giggles. Here's to the milestones, the memories, and the moments that make fatherhood the greatest adventure of all.

As you move through fatherhood, I hope you find your feet and thrive. Remember, you've got this. Parenthood may be the most challenging role you'll ever take on, but it's also the most rewarding. Embrace it fully, cherish it deeply, and savor every moment along the way.

BIBLIOGRAPHY

Blume, C., Garbazza, C., & Spitschan, M. (2019). Effects of light on human circadian rhythms, sleep and mood. *Somnologie, 23*(3), 147–156.
https://doi.org/10.1007/s11818-019-00215-x

Chechko, N., Dukart, J., Tchaikovski, S., Enzensberger, C., Neuner, I., & Stickel, S. (2021). The expectant brain—pregnancy leads to changes in brain morphology in the early postpartum period. *Cerebral Cortex, 32*(18), 4025–4038.
https://doi.org/10.1093/cercor/bhab463

Freeman, E., & Robinson, E. L. (2022). The relationship between father-child rough-and-tumble play and children's working memory. *Children (Basel), 9*(7), 962.
https://doi.org/10.3390/children9070962

İnce, T., Akman, H., Çımrın, D., & Aydın, A. (2018). The role of melatonin and cortisol circadian rhythms in the pathogenesis of infantile colic. *World Journal of Pediatrics, 14*(4), 392–398.
https://doi.org/10.1007/s12519-018-0130-1

Increased carrying reduces infant crying: a randomized controlled trial. (1986, May 1). PubMed.
https://pubmed.ncbi.nlm.nih.gov/3517799/

Kylie Rymanowicz, Michigan State University Extension. (2014, December 18). *Infant vision development: Helping babies see their bright futures!* MSU Extension.

https://www.canr.msu.edu/news/infant_vision_development_helping_babies_see_their_bright_futures#:~:text=Babies%20have%20an%20easier%20time,can%20encourage%20their%20vision%20development

Lucassen, P., Assendelft, W. J. J., Gubbels, J. W., Van Eijk, J., Van Geldrop, W. J., & Neven, A. K. (1998). Effectiveness of treatments for infantile colic: systematic review. *The BMJ*, *316*(7144), 1563–1569. https://doi.org/10.1136/bmj.316.7144.1563

McNamara, F., Lijowska, A. S., & Thach, B. T. (2002). Spontaneous arousal activity in infants during NREM and REM sleep. *The Journal of Physiology*, *538*(1), 263–269. https://doi.org/10.1113/jphysiol.2001.012507

Quante, M., McGee, G. W., Yu, X., Von Ash, T., Luo, M., Kaplan, E., Rueschman, M., Haneuse, S., Davison, K. K., Redline, S., & Taveras, E. M. (2022). Associations of sleep-related behaviors and the sleep environment at infant age one month with sleep patterns in infants five months later. *Sleep Medicine*, *94*, 31–37. https://doi.org/10.1016/j.sleep.2022.03.019

Skúladóttir, A., Thome, M., & Ramel, A. (2005). Improving day and night sleep problems in infants by changing day time sleep rhythm: a single group before and after study. *International Journal of Nursing Studies*, *42*(8), 843–850. https://doi.org/10.1016/j.ijnurstu.2004.12.004

Suni, E., & Suni, E. (2024, January 9). *Surprising ways hydration affects your sleep*. Sleep Foundation. https://www.sleepfoundation.org/nutrition/hydration-and-sleep

Tham, E. K., Schneider, N., & Broekman, B. F. (2017). Infant sleep and its relation with cognition and growth: a narrative review. *Nature and Science of Sleep, Volume 9*, 135–149. https://doi.org/10.2147/nss.s125992

Widström, A., Brimdyr, K., Svensson, K., Cadwell, K., & Nissen, E. (2019). Skin-to-skin contact the first hour after birth, underlying implications and clinical practice. *Acta Paediatrica, 108*(7), 1192–1204. https://doi.org/10.1111/apa.14754

Get Your Free Bonuses Now!

BONUS # 1: Survival Checklists for Dads
Your Key to Staying Organized and Making the Pregnancy Journey Super Smooth!

BONUS # 2: Mental Wellness Guide for Dads
Your Indispensable Guide to Self-care and Self-discovery, Ensuring a Journey Towards a Happier and More Fulfilled You!

BONUS # 3: Meditation Audio for Dads
Your Instant Escape to Calmness, Relaxation, and Well-deserved Quality "Me Time."

Scan with your phone's camera **OR** go to: https://bit.ly/43nFe2P

Made in the USA
Las Vegas, NV
11 November 2024